GRANDAD'S WAR

THE FIRST WORLD WAR DIARY OF HORACE REGINALD STANLEY

Compiled and edited by

Juliet Brodie (granddaughter) and
Heather Brodie (daughter)

First published in 2007 by
Poppyland Publishing, Cromer,
NR27 9AN
www.poppyland.co.uk

ISBN 978 0 946148 83 7

Designed & typeset in 11/14pt Times New Roman by Poppyland Publishing, Cromer NR27 9AN

Printed by Lightning Source.

Acknowledgements

We are extremely grateful to Mr Cliff Brown for his very helpful comments on the manuscript and for providing us with a range of information about the Cambridgeshire Regiment and some of the incidents recorded in the diary. We are also indebted to "Pop" (B.) and Sylvia Whitwell who have taken a great interest in the diary and invited us to see their collection of military memorabilia and share their knowledge and enthusiasm. We are also grateful for their hospitality. We also thank my former PhD student, Dr Mary Holmes, who very kindly scanned in the original black and white negatives that grandad had taken during the war. Finally, we acknowledge the contribution to this book from Peter Stibbons, whose input, particularly of present day photographs, has been a most valuable addition.

The Compilation and Editing Of The Diary

Horace Reginald Stanley's First World War diary spans the whole war and slightly beyond, commencing in July 1914 before the start of the war and ending in November 1918 plus a postscript written on his return to England after the war. My mother, Heather Brodie (HB) and I (JB) have transcribed the diary, undertaking very little editing except where we have felt it appropriate in terms of clarity. We have noted in the introduction that grandad rewrote half the diary at a later stage but here we present the original version owing to its immediacy and lack of his censorship. As a Sergeant in charge of a platoon, this diary gives a particular perspective. Grandad seemed to have a very special style of writing in the diary. He not only reported on the facts but he gave his thoughts and expressed his fears and at times it feels almost like a soliloquy. His writing is compelling and gripping. I personally think it is a remarkable piece of writing for a man who left school at 12. The diary is not written in chapters and we feel that it is better left as such. However, where possible, and particularly for the first part of the war, I have added (in italics) an indication of timing and events based on the record of the 1st Battalion The Cambridgeshire Regiment (to which grandad belonged until June 1915) during 1914-1919 (Riddell & Clayton, 1934). Mr Cliff Brown has also kindly commented on some of the timing and events in the diary and his observations can be found in the Appendix.

Juliet Brodie
April 2007

Contents

The web site *www.poppyland.co.uk* has a “Support and Resources” button which will lead to a number of pages specially compiled to support this title.

INTRODUCTION

Horace Reginald Stanley 1893-1971

Grandad served throughout the First World War, spending much of the time in France. His diary, which he kept throughout that time, is a remarkable account of the events that took place and of human survival. The diary was kept in the tank cupboard at his house and was not allowed to be read by his family. When his widow Eileen Stanley (neé Heffer) died in 1987 and the house in Cambridge was sold, the diary came to my mother, Heather Brodie (neé Stanley; my mother). We felt that it was such a remarkable account of the events that took place between 1914 and 1918 and because of the current state of interest in the subject that it should be made available to a wider audience. After the war, my grandfather rewrote about half the diary. He made alterations in places, often making parts more concise, but perhaps more interestingly applying a sort of censorship of activities that might have been deemed improper or offensive at that time. The first version, however, has an immediacy which is not so apparent in the revised version, so my mother and I have chosen to reproduce the original.

The contents of the diary are an insight into many aspects of war. Death, inevitably, in all its gruesome details is a frequent visitor. The apparent muddle of it all, the lack of ammunition and the impression that the British are totally on the defensive and just have to fight it out and maintain the line comes across throughout. But, it is the comments that are made, sometimes almost as a soliloquy or stream of consciousness that make this account so revealing. Here, the issue of men who could no longer face battle, deemed traitors at the time, is explored. Such men, apart from the braggarts, were not cowards or traitors in the eyes of grandad. He understands the absolute terror and can empathise. The concept of a living hell is all too real, but the aspects that make the war survivable for these men are also there: the relief to be able to delouse, the occasional pleasure of a good meal, the friendship of the local French families, the luxury of a proper lavatory. There are funny and poignant parts and perhaps the saddest of the little dog that was too fond of the drink and came to a sticky end.

I think for grandad the homecomings were as bad and sad as being in France. The attitude of the people back home ranged from despising him for having survived when so many others had not, to thinking that they must have been having a fine old time out there. There did not seem to be any gratitude for these people who had risked their lives for King and country.

Biography of Horace Reginald Stanley

In 1958, after 52½ years in the industry, Horace Reginald Stanley retired from the staff of the Cambridge Gas Company and spent a quiet retirement with his wife, Florence Eileen Stanley in Cambridge, where he had spent all his life apart from his time in France during the First World War. In an article on his retirement in the Eastern Gas News, April 1958, my grandfather was described as "One of the best known figures among the staff of the Cambridge Division whose reputation extends far beyond its boundaries...". He was also recognized for his undoubted talent and initiative and for his ability and energy. It was, however, his experiences in the First World War and the remarkable diary that he wrote during that time that provide a detailed insight into the man and must have had a profound impact on him for the rest of his life.

Grandad, Sergeant Stanley, pictured in the Eastern Gas house magazine on his retirement from the company.

Grandad was born towards the end of the 19th Century, the second son of Emily (neé Willis) and Charles Stanley (a Chesterton man) who had three more children, Frederick, the oldest child, Sarah Florence ("Auntie Florrie"), who was born after grandad and the last child, another daughter who died aged three when recovering from diphtheria. Grandad's childhood appears to have been a mixture of responsibility, fun and mischief without malice, plus experimentation. He would collect blackberries and mushrooms and other "fruits" of the country for his mother and work on the allotment to feed the family. He knew how to graft cultivated roses onto wild briars and would create such mixtures in the countryside to cause surprise to passers by. He kept an animal hospital and knew how to tend sick and stray animals, who seemed to find his home, and mend broken wings of birds. When experiments into psychic research were being undertaken in Cambridge, he and his friends would secretly set up hauntings and they would also tie people's door knockers together, knock and run away. He also experimented with explosives and one day he blew a hole in his mother's house! These skills he developed in childhood would almost certainly have helped his survival in the trenches.

Sometime between the death of the last daughter and grandad starting work, their father left the family for good, severing all contact and leaving their mother to raise the three remaining children on her own. No one knows why their father left the family and it appears to have been a taboo subject, but Auntie Florrie in later years occasionally spoke fondly of her father and the happy times before he left. It is possible to surmise that after the death of the last child, it was all too much for Emily and ultimately the marriage. We don't know very much at all about Emily, other than what we can perhaps infer from the diary. When grandad visits her (p. 49) after recovering from illness, he writes "Mother looks older and grayer. I can see what she is suffering, a suffering which neither money nor food can assuage." Later (p. 70), after the death of his brother Frederick, when he goes on leave he writes "My mother is broken with sorrow and deep in a lethargy which cannot be lifted. I should not have come home, it would have been better otherwise." Emily is clearly a woman who is unable to hide her emotions and despair and who might be described as suffering from a deep depression from which she never really recovered. I can't help feeling that she was similarly affected by the death of her second daughter.

Brother Frederick Stanley in a studio portrait.

The three children were clever and would have gone to the grammar school at the appropriate age but special permission was sought for them not to continue at school as they needed to work to provide an income for the family. Emily is known to have had to take in washing to make money at some stage to provide for the family. Frederick became an apprentice tailor. During the war he joined the army but he was not called up until Spring 1918. He had a wife and family to support at this stage. Again, the diary is an insight into grandad's brother. It's almost as if grandad has a premonition that if Frederick goes to war then he will not survive. During the same visit when he is recovering from illness that provides an insight into his mother (p. 49), he writes: "I enquire of my brother, he too is a soldier, a married man with a family. He has not gone to war yet and I am glad. He is impetuous and of a fateful disposition and the last time I saw him I seemed to detect the same look I saw in the eyes of the fellow that stopped a bullet at the Brasserie. I hope he won't have to go." Frederick did end up going to France in 1918 and was almost immediately killed on the 21st March when his dug-out received a direct hit somewhere near Arras. His body was never found but his name[2] is recorded on a bay at the Faubourg-D'Amiens Cemetery, a sad but beautiful and peaceful memorial at Arras, designed by Lutyens and much visited by descendants of those listed there. Grandad writes (p. 69): "My brother is dead. He probably had his back to the wall[6]. It is of no use to moan. Every other soldier wears a black button now. Could we but return to the happy days of 1914, things can never be the same again, my brother is dead. I expected this but my poor old mother she will never be the same again. I may not even see her again."

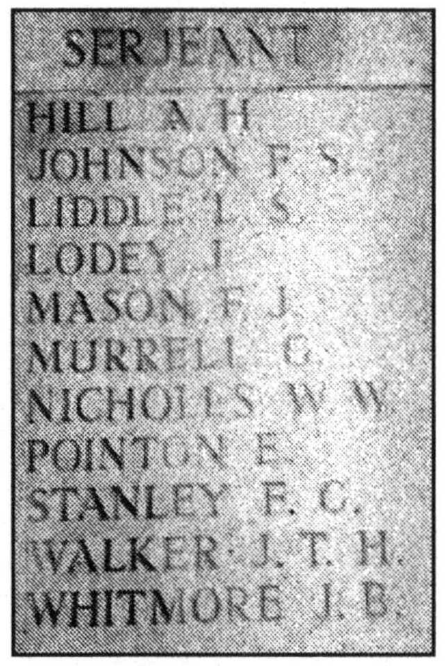

Frederick's name on the Arras monument.

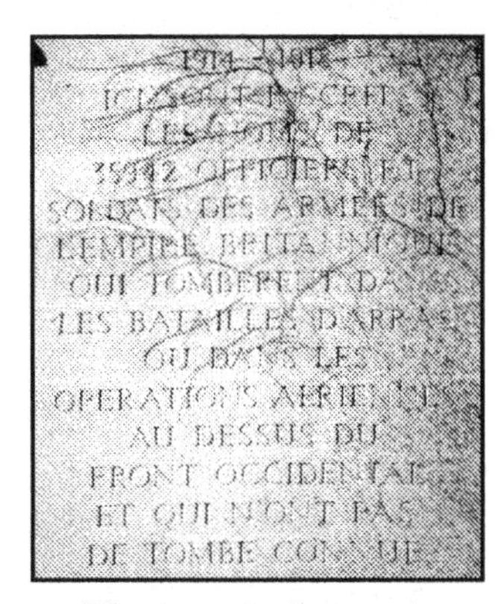

The inscription at Arras for those "with no known grave".

Auntie Florrie took a certificate in shop keeping and after the war, grandad gave her the money to buy a grocer's shop in Cambridge which she ran until she retired. She never married, despite having admirers and her special male friend with whom she enjoyed amateur dramatics and activities connected with the Church. She was good fun and an interesting great aunt to me. She loved her garden, singing in the choir in the Round Church, her ginger cat and was an excellent needle woman; she struck me as an independent, somewhat emancipated woman who had been affected by what had happened to her mother when their father left. She also had a careful streak that was rather amusing and you couldn't really describe it as mean but I can see it in other members of the family and assume it is a genetic trait. So, if for afternoon tea when my two brothers and I were visiting with grandad and granny there was a pint of jelly that would have to go around six people, a portion would always be put away in the larder to be saved for another occasion, or a mini pork pie cut into thin slices.

Grandad, like Frederick, was due to take up work as a tailor at the age of 12 in 1905, but after a week of sitting crossed legged, decided that it was not for him. So he took himself to the Gas Company at 41 Sidney Street, Cambridge and demanded work from the manager, Mr. Auchterlonie who told the young boy "Go home to your mother, laddie". But grandad said that he must have work and he was taken on as a messenger whose duties included running errands to scrubbing floors. Shortly after this time the Gas Company moved to larger premises at 52 Sidney Street (at the time of writing now Lakeland Plastics outlet) and at 13, Horace became a gas fitter's apprentice, starting work at 6 am and working 56 hours a week. He also studied three evenings a week at the Cambridge School of Arts and Crafts and one evening a week at the Cavendish Laboratory studying gas supply and related subjects. His industriousness enabled him to be awarded the City and Guilds of London examination in gas supply.

When he was 14, grandad - we think almost certainly unofficially - joined the Cambridge University Rifle Volunteers (which became the Officers' Training Corps) as a drummer. He chose to be a drummer boy in order to enjoy summer camp in Windsor Great Park. He joined the

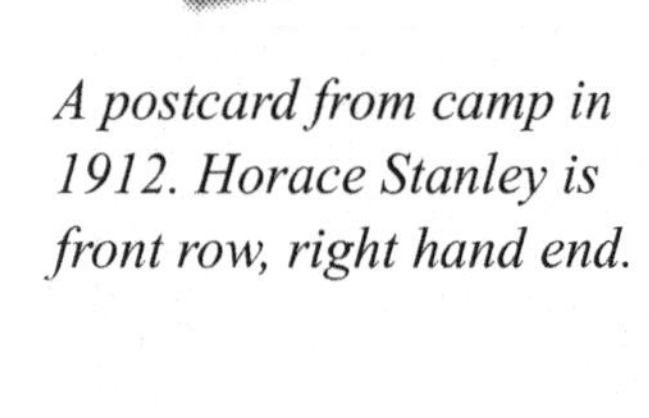
POST CARD.

A postcard from camp in 1912. Horace Stanley is front row, right hand end.

1st Cambridgeshire Regiment on 4th March 1909. The Cambridgeshire Regiment, T.F. (Territorial Force) was a military unit composed of civilians, as part of the new volunteer force. It had a continuous history as a unit of the non-professional army from 1860-1914. For additional details of the Regiment, including the line of descent and details of its forerunner, the 30th Foot (Cambridgeshire) which originated in 1702, see Riddell & Clayton (1934) and Macdonald (1998).

In 1913 grandad was a Private in the Regiment in C company. At this time there were eight companies, A to H. By 5th August 1914, he was mobilised to serve as a volunteer with the 1st Battalion Cambridgeshire Regiment for Imperial Service (i.e. to serve abroad at this stage), by which time he was a Lance Corporal. Between 24th November and 5th December 1914 he undertook a special course in musketry at the School of Musketry Bisley Camp where he passed as a 1st Class Instructor. In January 1915, the 1st Battalion changed to a four company system: A and B amalgamated to form A company, C and D to form B company and so on. On 14th February 1915, grandad went to France with the battalion, by which time he was a Sergeant in B company, No 6 platoon, No. 8 section and responsible for 13 other men. At this time, the commanding officer of 5, 6, 7 and 8 platoons of B company was Major E.T. Saint and second in command Captain O. Tebbutt.

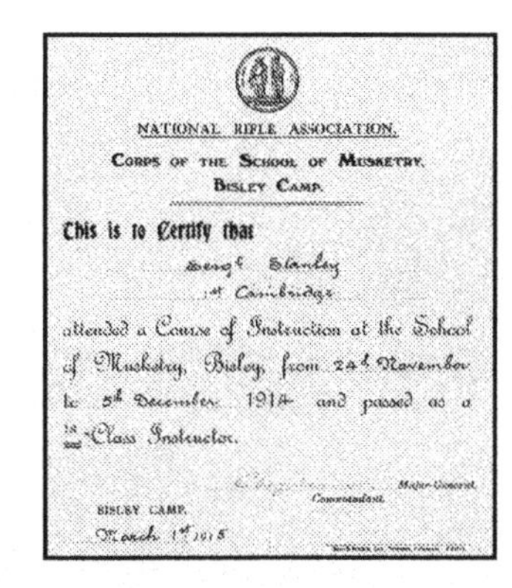

NATIONAL RIFLE ASSOCIATION.

CORPS OF THE SCHOOL OF MUSKETRY.
BISLEY CAMP.

This is to Certify that

Sergt Stanley
1st Cambridge

attended a Course of Instruction at the School of Musketry, Bisley, from 24th November to 5th December 1914 and passed as a 1st Class Instructor.

[illegible] Major-General
Commandant.

BISLEY CAMP.
March 1st 1915

A successful course at Bisley in 1914.

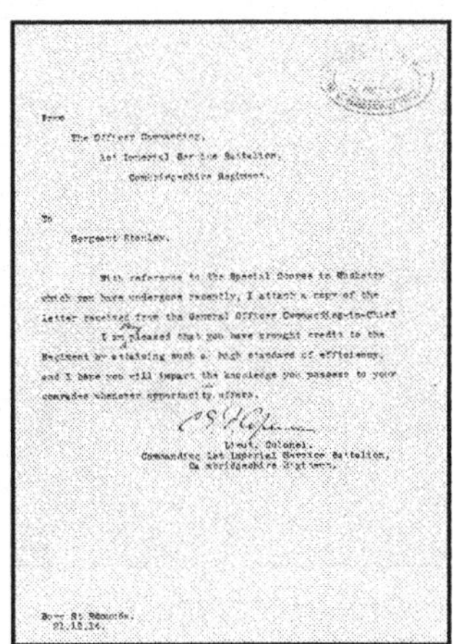

From

The Officer Commanding,
1st Imperial Service Battalion,
Cambridgeshire Regiment.

To

Sergeant Stanley.

With reference to the Special Course in Musketry which you have undergone recently, I attach a copy of the letter received from the General Officer Commanding-in-Chief.

I am very pleased that you have brought credit to the Regiment by attaining such a high standard of efficiency, and I hope you will impart the knowledge you possess to your comrades whenever opportunity offers.

[illegible]
Lieut. Colonel.
Commanding 1st Imperial Service Battalion,
Cambridgeshire Regiment.

Bury St Edmunds.
21.12.14.

Commendation from the Commanding Officer.

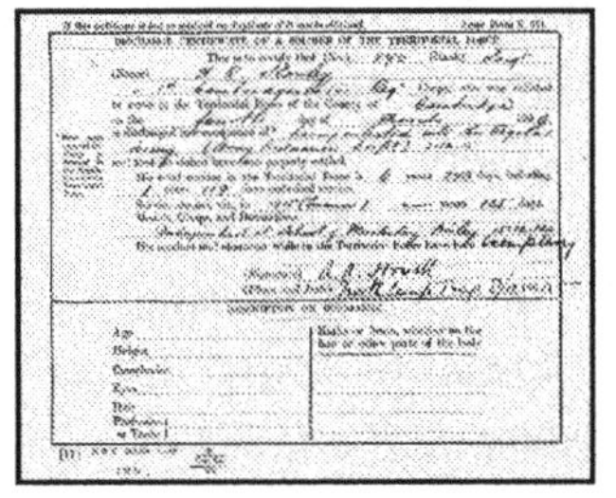

Discharge from the Territorials to go into the Regular Army.

The sergeants of the 3/1st Cambridgeshire Regiment, November 1915.

Back row, left to right: J.Gerrard, H.Stanley, H.Pull, A.Humberstone, P.Hall, G.Stoakley, P.Stubbins, H.Bigg, A.Ashman.
Middle row: J.Hurry, W.Lawrence, L.Stoakley, E.Hotson, W.Westley, H.Hunt, H.Knott, F.Rowe.
Front row: C.Walton, P.Cornwell, A.Warner, J.Utteridge, W.Freeman, F.Parker

He served with the Regiment for 125 days in France until June 1915 when he returned home unwell. When he recovered he spent time with the 3/1st batallion in Windsor and Tring. On 2nd December 1915 grandad was discharged from the Regiment in order to enlist into the Regular Army where he became a member of the Army Ordnance Corps. He was repeatedly asked to become an officer, but knew the Mess would be a temptation and he needed to send money home and he cared for the welfare of the ordinary man.

During the war grandad saw front line service as a Sergeant, taking part in a number of famous engagements, including the battles of St. Eloi and Ypres, before and throughout the first gas battles for the Channel Ports. After he was drafted to the Regular Army at the end of 1915, he served in France and Belgium until the cease fire on 11th November 1918. During July 1918 he was selected for a commission as a Flying Officer but owing to the trend of the war and its termination this did not develop. His gallant and distinguished service during the war was acknowledged. After the war in March 1919 he was mentioned in a despatch from Field Marshall Sir Douglas Haig which

The Cambridgeshire Platoons

- 5 platoon consisted of sections 1-4. The commanding officer was Lt R.J. Tebbutt and the platoon Sergeant was H.C. Clarke.
- 6 platoon [grandad's platoon], 5-8 sections, Lt V.G.L. Mallet (later Lt E.H. Hopkinson), Sgt H. Pull.
- 7 platoon, 9-12 sections, Lt H.C. Few, Sgt G.H. Mann.
- 8 platoon, 13-16 sections, Lt K.C. Gill, Sgt E.C. Aves.

Soldiers in Number 6 platoon 8 section

Sgt H.R. Stanley, No 841	
Pte H.W. Lander, 1414	Wounded 10.5.1915.
Pte W. Roberts, 2404	Wounded 10.5.1915.
Pte H. Spencer, 2616	Wounded June and September 1916 and 13.11.1916.
Pte E. Pierson, 1975	Killed in Action 4.9.1916.
Pte L.A. Maxim, 2985	Wounded 28.9.1916 and 31.7.1917.
Pte J. Sindle, 2633	Wounded 10.6.1915; died of wounds 20.6.1915.
Pte G. Sutton, 2633	Killed in Action, 3 12.1916.
Pte H.C. Talbot, 2570	Wounded 10.8.1916.
Pte J. Monel, 2559	Missing 21-31.3.1918; Prisoner of War.
Pte T. Newton, 3004	Invalided with trench fever September 1916.
Pte S. Lilley, 3006	
Pte C. Dye, 2594	Wounded 31.7.1917.
Pte B. Phillips, 2176	Killed in Action.

Sergeant Stanley labelled this photograph "The Old Brags". It was probably taken during their first winter in France; one soldier sports a captured enemy helmet but the British soldiers have not yet been issued with helmets. Another wears a sheepskin over his uniform.

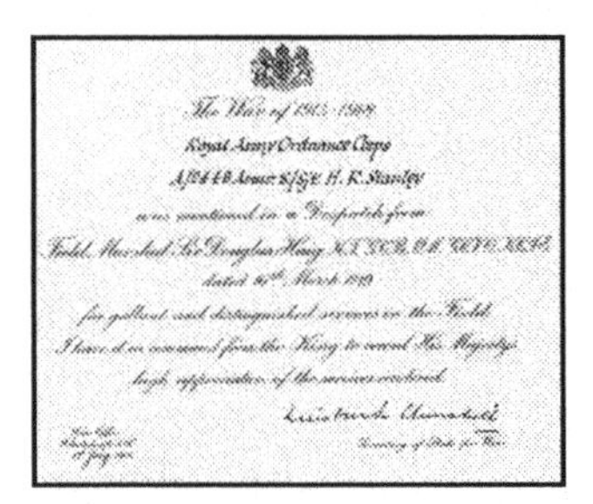
Royal Army Ordnance Corps
was mentioned in a Despatch from
Field Marshal Sir Douglas Haig
for gallant and distinguished services in the Field.

Mentioned in despatches, with a signature from Winston Churchill.

was signed by Winston Churchill, Secretary of State for War at the time. Grandad was demobilised from France during May 1919 and returned to duty with the Cambridge University and Town Gas Light Company.

After demobilisation, grandad returned to the Gas Company workshops in Sidney Street as a gas fitter and went on to pass the City and Guilds final examination in gas fitting with distinction. He was also awarded the Institute's silver medal. He went on to pass the British Commercial Gas Association's Course in Salemanship also with distinction. In due course he was appointed chief outside representative closely followed by promotion to gas superintendent, the position he held until he retired. The E.G. News[1] article at the time of his retirement in 1958 states that "Courtesy, courage, and the desire to be helpful were his main attributes, and nothing seemed too much trouble. It is with such a testimony and an enviable record of achievements that he bid farewell to his life's work, a credit to his own day and generation and an example to those who come after."

At his time at 52 Sidney Street he lived above the Gas Showrooms with granny and their three children. Grandad could see Christ's Pieces from his bedroom and could hear the singing of the birds as he woke up in the morning.
My mother recalls the fabulous parties she and her brother and sister had on birthdays and at Christmas above the showrooms and how some of her friends have recently returned to remember the old days and at least to make it to what was the boardroom on the second floor.

A formal portrait of Horace Stanley after the war; for a senior N.C.O. to survive throughout the war on active service on the western front was not unknown but experienced by all too few.

THE DIARY

Prior to the start of the war, in July 1914 the Territorial Battalions of the Cambridgeshire Regiment were at Ashridge Park for their annual training.

July 1914 and the Territorial Battalions are doing their annual training in camp. The atmosphere is warm in more senses than one for a great crisis is at hand, how great we do not appreciate, for what does youth care of political intrigues, besides, war has been in the air for years but has never got beyond the talking stage and newspaper scares, and what if it does come, for youth it means adventure, romance, honour and glory. The days slip by and rumour follows rumour and there is tension everywhere, and a distinct difference is noticed in our training. We are taught extended order and trench digging and general field operations, the Medical Officer lectures upon sanitation, and quotes figures from past campaigns. We are also taught first aid and stretcher work, all ominous signs but nevertheless it is a great joke and nobody seems to be perturbed about the whole thing. Towards the end of the camp we are told that war is probable and what a cheer goes up, what waving of hats and what comments of how we will thrash the Germans, how we will mow them down with our superior marksmanship when they attack in massed formation as we are told they will. Yes we have arranged everything. We will let them get nearly upon us and then open rapid fire and those that do not fall or run away we will get among with the bayonet and practise the clean walk through opposition as taught by our instructor: a thrust forward with the bayonet, a sharp withdrawal at the same time bringing up the right foot and kicking the opponent in the stomach and as he bends forward in pain, thrust the butt of the rifle under his chin, then bash it down on his head and ready for the next one. What glory! But one must not let ones imagination run away too much for upon thinking things over some of us would probably get wounded or even perhaps killed. We will buy the old soldiers among us some beer and perhaps they will tell us more, but I notice they will not talk seriously of their experiences and now the first excitement has subsided they do not seem so excited about the prospects of war as us youngsters. Surely they were not afraid, these old warriors of former campaigns. They just seem to smile a cynical, sideways kind of smile which seems to say we know but we do not tell. I don't like it.

On 4th August, 1914, the Commanding Officer of the Cambridgeshire Regiment, Lieutenant-Colonel Louis Tebbutt, received a telegram to mobilise. On 5th August 1914 the Cambridgeshire Regiment was mobilised.

August 1914

It is now August 1914 and who having lived through these days can forget it. The camp has broken up and we are back at our old jobs in civil life. The hoarders and profiteers are busy all ready, prices have risen and certain commodities are getting scarce. If things are so bad with rumours of war, it is terrible to think what will happen if war does come, and I like others must prepare, for I cannot leave my poor old mother to starve whilst I am away fighting. A friend can get me a sack of flour at a special price. I must get it. We have plenty of potatoes and the thirty pounds saved in the Post Office must be withdrawn while there is yet the chance. This will suffice until Christmas and everybody says that if hostilities commence now our Navy will starve out the Germans before Christmas if we do not beat them in the field before that time comes. What fools we poor mortals are.

August Bank Holiday. We must make the most of this for we are already heroes, fêted by our friends wherever we go. This is strange for a short while ago we were jeered at as toy soldiers, and treated as a joke and in many cases free fights and street fracas ensued but this is all changed now and we are going to show them that we are ready and can really fight like real soldiers.

Tuesday back at work again, the holiday being over, but precious little work is being done for War is on every tongue and the manager coming upon a group informs them that mobilisation has been ordered, and he is the most serious of all. Perhaps he is older, the men appear highly delighted at this opportunity to show their prowess.

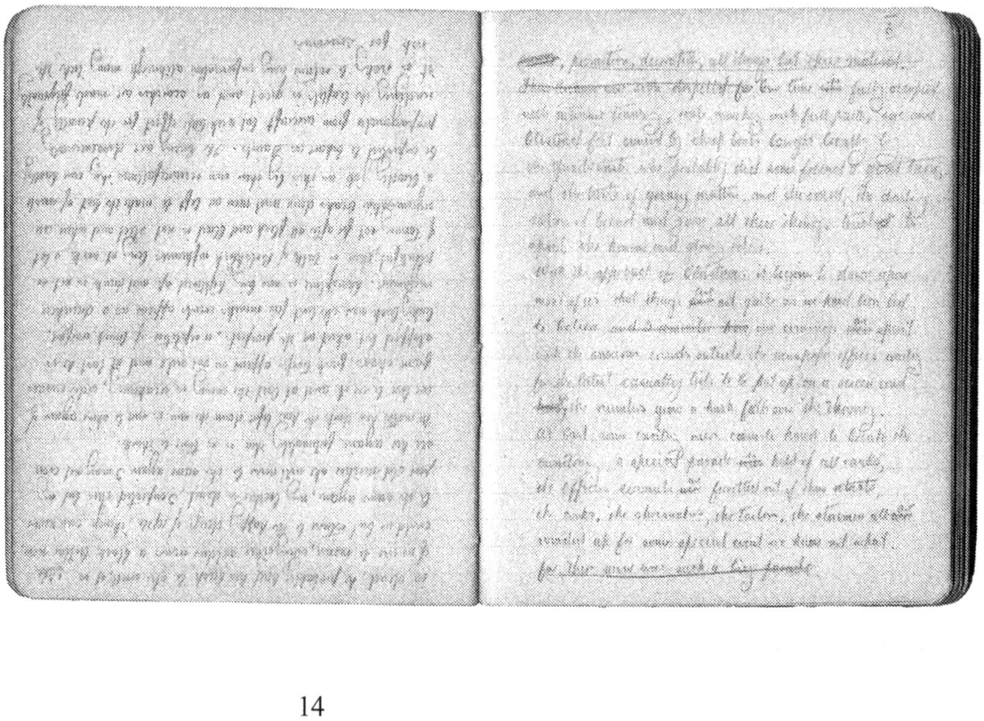

Sergeant Stanley's diary. He wrote through the book on the right hand pages, turned it over once complete and wrote again on the right hand page. Consequently here we have his page 6 one way up and his page 134 the other way up.

Our time is now fully occupied with intensive training, route marching with full pack, sore and blistered feet caused by cheap boots bought locally by the quartermaster who probably did some friend a good turn, and the taste of greasy mutton and the smell, the daily ration of bread and jam, all these things tend to spoil the honour and glory idea. With the approach of Christmas it begins to dawn upon most of us that things are not quite as we had been led to believe. Our evenings are spent with the anxious crowds outside the newspaper offices waiting for the latest casualty lists to be put up on a screen; eager eyes scan the casualty lists and as the numbers grow a hush falls over the throng. At last exciting news comes to hand to break the monotony. A special parade is called of all ranks. The Officers' servants are ferreted out of their retreats, the cooks, the shoemakers, tailors and the storeman are all rounded up for the great parade. After all the details of falling in, dressing and redressing etc, and all the irksome repetitions, the Colonel takes over the parade and after explaining the reverses of our Regular Army in France and Belgium [the struggle on the Western Front] and this great thing our country is up against, he makes a strong appeal for volunteers to fight at once. Here a striking psychological study presents itself - one of the first volunteers is a small insignificant little man who has many times been the butt of those of finer physique. Who would connect such courage with this little man? Here is an example of patriotism and the urge to rally to his sorely pressed comrades over the channel. Then a few more join him, mere boys who have given a wrong age to enlist and a cook who has flat feet and looks none too robust. I cannot understand it at all. What has become of that fine dashing Officer, he of the spurs and leggings and a firm figure and that strong silent instructor who has taught us to frighten the Germans first before killing them and those fine fellows with tight fitting uniforms the admiration of the ladies? We cannot fight without them. Why are they not with us? We indeed look a scruffy crew. Perhaps the others will change their minds and join us later. Some do but many do not.

The Cambridgeshire Regiment convoy set out on the 14th February for Southampton and disembarked in Le Havre the following morning.

Great changes are now taking place, those who decided to fight are separated from those who decide to wait, our numbers are gradually strengthened by drafts of recruits and our training becomes more intensive and at last we steal away one morning for Southampton there to embark on the transports for Havre.

By this time there is a strong feeling of comradeship, everybody seems full of jollity and good spirits, we are really going to be of some use and every hour brings some new experience and how excited everyone seems there when at dawn the coast of France comes into view. How strange

A quick and unofficial photograph as the troop ship reaches Le Havre.

these French people seem, quite a novelty with their chatter and gestures and how insistent the children with their cries of "Souvenir", "Bully Biff" and a lot of gabble which we cannot understand, and so, cheered by the populace as we march to the base camp we give lusty vent to some of our favourite marching songs. Our speciality, one of these a very vulgar edition, meets with great approval from the daughters of France who swing along with us. It refers to the exploits of a German officer and goes like this:

A German Officer crossed the Rhine parlez vous.
A German Officer crossed the Rhine parlez vous.
All he wanted was women and wine
Hinky pinky parlez vous.

O landlord have you a daughter fine parlez vous.
O landlord have you a daughter fine parlez vous.
O landlord have you a daughter fine fit for an officer of the line
Hinky pinky parlez vous.

My daughter sir is far too young parlez vous...

But that good reader is enough for as the lines increase so the tone gets lower.

Between 15th February and 16th March 1915 the Regiment undertook some training and made their way towards the front line at St. Eloi. There was time for writing and some unofficial photography.

It is February and the camp is covered with snow fast melting as it falls, turning the ground into a marsh aided by the tramp of many feet, and at night one is glad to crowd into a bell tent and sleep like a sardine close between one's fellows to steal a little welcome warmth from one another as fires are not allowed in camp. Further along the hillside are camped the Gurkhas, small thin brown men of whom we have heard such bloodcurdling reports of how they would steal into the enemy trenches at night and with their fearsome knives sever the heads of the Germans as they stood and bring them back for souvenirs. In spite of these reports they are quite harmless and anxious to exchange small trinkets for souvenirs. They are housed in warm huts more fortunate than ourselves and complain bitterly of the cold. One could not help feeling that the powers had blundered badly in bringing them to face the rigours of a campaign in this cold damp country when they could have been employed on other fronts in a climate more suited to their temperament.

A day and a night packed in a cattle truck brings us nearer to the line of battle. When the allotted number of men are packed in these trucks with their equipment and rations, things are all right while they remain standing but one cannot do this for a day and a

From the men who were there. Sergeant Stanley's diary entry for February 1915 and one of the maps prepared by Brigadier-General Riddell and Colonel Clayton to illustrate their later account of the history of the Cambridgeshires from 1914 to 1919.

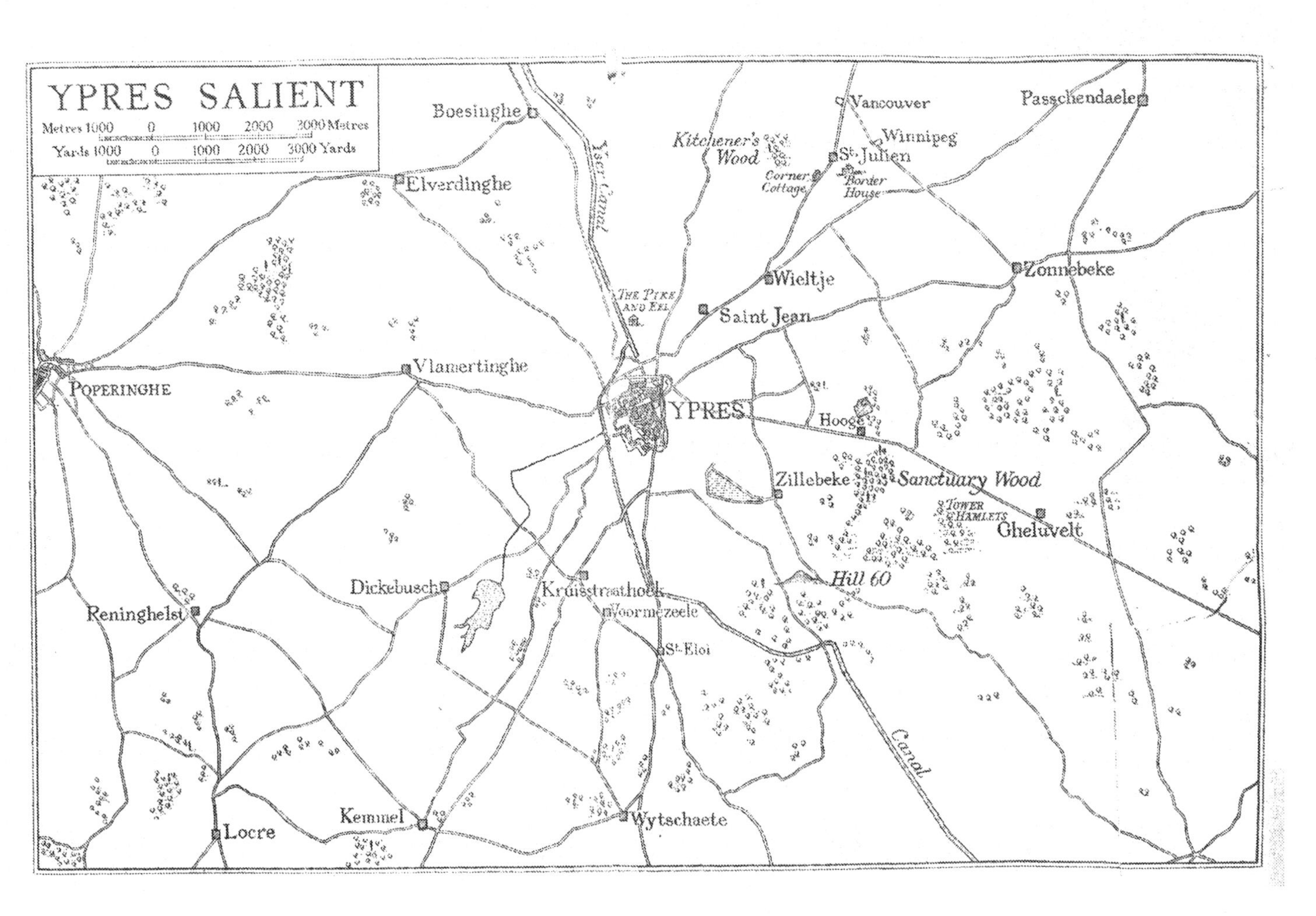

Sergeant Stanley made good use of his camera as time permitted in periods behind the lines, giving us a remarkable record, somewhat different to most World War One imagery. These pictures probably come from his later service with the Army Ordnance Corps.

night so after a lot of shuffling a fairly comfortable position can be gained. Some play cards, either winning or losing what money they have. This is not much for it was not at this time known that money could be spent near the fighting line. Some sit on the footboards watching the landscape slowly pass but soon tiring of this. There is a general cursing when in finding a more comfortable position somebody's mess tin is upset after nearly an hours effort in trying to brew a cup of tea with the aid of a piece of rifle flannel dipped in a tin lid full of rifle oil or any odd piece of fat that can be scrounged.

A few more days marching from farm to farm where the nights are spent in comfortable barns and we find ourselves in a small canvas camp in a copse near Dickebush where the guns and rifle fire can be distinctly heard and at night the skyline in the direction of the front is illuminated intermittently by the Verey lights. Having a few hours leisure before nightfall we take a stroll into the village and to our surprise children are playing unconcernedly in the streets and shops are doing business as usual. The drinking houses are well patronised by a few troops with a little leisure like ourselves. Turning a corner we come upon a dressing station and a cemetery and seeing troops digging rows of what are undoubtedly graves, we ask a Corporal what the idea is and after cadging a cigarette he answers in a matter of fact way "We like to bury `em decently when we gets the chance and there's a do coming off to-night". At that moment a loud thud followed by an ear splitting explosion occurs and everybody ducks. Just behind us a miniature volcano bursts forth followed by a shower of mud and stones with pieces of whistling shell which seems to fall for a long time. All eyes turn to the Corporal and all voices seem to say as one "What's that?" "Garn" said he "whose leg are you pullin'?" But, I explained, we have just arrived from England. "Oh have yer, well that's a lump of Jerry's junk" which we took to mean is a German shell. "But don't they do any damage" said I, for the party still work on digging. "No they're harmless enough if yer don't get too close to em, a coalbox dropped in that Engineers' dump over there last week, we found most of the pieces and buried em". Just there on the left and sure enough was a rough wooden cross with six names written on with blue pencil surmounted by the words R· I· P. We do not want the Corporal to think we are afraid as we give him some more cigarettes but I feel anxious to get a move on and make the excuse that we have to get back to camp, for if another shell comes along it might fall a trifle short.

At dusk the Platoon assembles and proceeds to a dump where a guide is allotted and off we go. We do not know where, or for what, for we are located like a lot of school children, but what does it matter so long as we just follow my leader, get a belly full of food of sorts, and some cigarettes. We do not march now as we have done for months which seemed months of left right, left right, but just amble along in single file, all kinds of messages being passed from one to the other, "hole on right, stump on left, wires etc.", the whole thing being good fun. After about an hour we arrive at what was once a brewery, the upper part now in ruins. It appears to be a store and stands at cross roads.

We are loaded with picks and shovels, a bundle of sandbags, bundles of barbed wire, stakes, mallets and all kinds of gadgets and when we are served we wait for a fresh guide. It is an inky black night with just a nip in the air and as we squat around waiting the conversation turns on many topics. One fellow seems a little dejected, he has been for some time. He thinks he is for it and his very presence seems to shout it aloud. I remember when in England sleeping five in a line in a narrow room when throwing some object out of the window he broke a mirror and from that time he seemed to get worse, and although he is a splendid fellow with a fine stock of courage, he cannot shift this obsession and tonight his conversation and general manner seems to forbode some ill omen. Some of the fellows laugh.

The town of Dickebush is grouped around its church. The Old Military Cemetery, probably on the site of the dressing station to which Sergeant Stanley refers, is in the centre of the town, beside the church. A little out of town is the étang, the lake, with its café and pump house - familiar to the troops of 1914 and 1915 as a delousing station and no doubt a place where a little fishing could be undertaken.

It is weird to-night, everything is so quiet, when we started we could hear the firing but now it has entirely ceased and but for the firework display in the distance and this peculiar ghostly feeling the world might be at peace. The boys, becoming a little impatient, are crooning a favourite ditty -

> The bells of hell went ting-a-ling-a ling
> For you but not for me
> O death where is thy sting-a-ling-a-ling
> O grave thy victory

A voice with a brogue which leaves no doubt of the country of its origin quietens them. "For the love of Moike, will yez be after the loikes of kaping quiet and putting out yez cigarettes."
Another voice from the darkness: "What's' the matter Pat, have you got the wind up?"
"The divil a bit its not only yez loife theyre after the loikes of wanting but yez loife blood intoirely intoirely".
A wag expresses the thought, under cover of the darkness: "Pat you have bats in the belfry my lad."
Lucky for the wag it is dark but for a few moments the air is filled with curses "Be Jasus and yey'll remember the words of an old Oirishman who'll be lucky if he ever draws his pension." and as the word comes to prepare to move off, and Pat gives a parting reminder "If yez put yez head round the corner they'll snipe the head off yez.", and off we go round the corner of the old Brasserie in single file with our burdens, keeping in touch with our guide. A weird sharp phut!, a sound like driving a nail into a soft brick, a ghostly moan followed by a gurgling long drawn out groan of pain and the word passes, man hit, it is the fellow who was expecting it and he has it properly in the stomach. After being bandaged and put on a stretcher. I peered through the darkness into his face and the look still there - no hope. He died next day and the Corporal at the dressing station had another new tenant for one of his holes. This first impression had rather a nauseating effect upon me. I remember now the smell of warm, steaming blood and as the stretcher bearers lifted him none too gently the blood can be heard dripping to the ground like rain dripping from a broken gutter. No flash was observed and the bullet

did not come from the direction of the line, it must have been the sniper that Pat had warned us of. It is depressing and with no means of retaliation. The going is heavy now and makes one sweat, the joking gives way to cursing and swearing, "hole on right", the parrot cry passed along but before one had passed it on, too late, you are in it up to the waist, mud that stinks and sticks like glue, "wires", and before there is time to duck, your head is nearly pulled off your shoulders. "Stump on left", your shins are scraped and the fellows in the rear stumble and fall whilst the oncoming fellow treads on your hands and face. A treacherous crack spits out spasmodically and bullets whistle and whine overhead making eerie noises as they strike the sapless branches of the trees, some at a lower angle phut phutting into the trunks, others ricocheting like a lot of imprisoned spirits struggling to be free of their fetters.

As we skirt the edge of the wood we are told to go quietly and whenever a Verey light is observed to remain motionless until it is dark again. The bullets seem to whistle incessantly now close over our heads, and we require no advice to keep cover, in fact most of the rest of the journey is spent with our bellies very close to the cold, muddy ground. It is now necessary to reach our objective to wait until it is dark and dash across some open ground. A favourable moment arrives and off we go. No sooner have we started, however, than up goes a Verey light and down we go. These cursed lights are uncanny. They seem to start off with a pouf and then as though suspended by invisible wires they seem to rest in mid air for an interminable time throwing up all kinds of grotesque objects, some probably figments of a distraught imagination. With face buried in the mud one dare not look up or move a muscle or even look for fear of detection, and a physical fear which seems to turn the stomach into a vacuum and when I think of that poor fellow who was hit in the stomach at the Brasserie, and sweat breaks out on me, how happy I should feel if I were seated on a comfortable lavatory. Darkness again, as I raise my head and put out my hand. It touches something cold and stiff and as my eyes become accustomed to the darkness the outline of a face appears. I try to look away, I struggle to rise but some fear forces me to look closer. Two holes appear, the nostrils and eyes, the skin stretched over the cheek bones. It is death! Death! It seems to smile but its eyes are fixed. "Who are you"? The sudden challenge brings its power back to my limbs and feeling something which feels like a bayonet pressing against my ribs, I struggle to speak "Friend!". "Friend be b...., who are you?" I stuttered the name of my Regiment. "Well what's your game, your pals are over there." "My god but look at that face he is dead!" "Oh there's lots of them sods laying around here. There's lots of them laying about, we mopping `em up, no communication here and perhaps get Blighty for our trouble." Anyway we get an extra issue of S.R.D., you slip over with him to his crowd Nobby he's got the wind up. Keeps yer bowels well open sonny and trust in the Lord you'll soon get used to it if you don't get a souvenir."

The next two hours are spent filling sandbags and placing them as directed by the Engineers. We are told it is to be a machine gun post, and in front others are driving in wood stakes and making a network of barbed wire, when we are told to follow the guide back to the Brasserie, no man wants telling twice. When the tools are handed in at the dump, we gather again under the old Brasserie wall and smoke a cigarette, we are more cautious now and conceal all lights. "Well says the guide I'm glad to be out of that bloody hole for another night I thought we were going to get it in the neck to-night, it seems too quiet to be healthy but I think the bastards had a skinful last night when the Irish caught them coming through." But I ask where is the Boche and where are our soldiers and the fighting, for none was apparent. " The Boche was about a hundred yards in front of the wire where you fellows were putting up to-night, you've heard of No Man's Land haven't you! Well that where we've been to-night and every night out there. Puts years on a man's life until he sooner or later gets a Blighty, goes mad or lays out there to rot or feed to the rats. That's a bad spot and we are trying to improve it." "But where are the trenches?" "Oh there are plenty of trenches but they don't connect here and Jerry comes through sometimes and has a look around, I daresay in a few years time they'll dig some trenches here when they get enough troops to put in them." "But why don't they go for each other and fight?" " Taint good for yer, if you've got a gun in a snug little billet, keep it there until it's wanted that is if you don't want a flying pig to come on top of you and turn you out."

We are now back resting in a small town and apart from the rumble of the line things are quite good. In fact after the first experience of the front this seems a perfect paradise. We are billeted in some derelict houses where we settle down and make ourselves quite comfortable. At night persistent mice travel over my face and nibble my rations, even entering the pockets of my greatcoat and searching for crumbs. This one does not mind but when they have the audacity to make holes in one's emergency ration bags something has to be done. The next day the holes are filled with pieces of glass, old razor blades and nails, but even this does not prevent their invasion so a further scheme is tried with more success. The bread rations when removed from the sandbags used to carry it in usually had a growth of whiskers gathered from the sides of the bags and when bread was plentiful the crust was sliced off and thrown away so this was rammed down all the holes as tight as possible and my theory is that the mice, in eating their way through the bread became so well fed that they fell asleep over the task.

Resting between actions. The uniforms suggest that it is from Sergeant Stanley's later serivce with the Army Ordnance Corps.

We are usually aroused in the mornings by peasant girls hawking new laid eggs, these girls pick their way among the recumbent troops soon disposing of their wares, they can be heard coming over the cobbled roads with clogs clattering in

Doing the laundry.

the morning air and cries of "Trés bon oeufs", "Trés bon oeufs". The troops carry on a jocular repartee with an element of smut and it is generally agreed that one fair damsel brings some very fine eggs and cheap, referred to in general parlance bloody fine eggs. She is a very apt pupil and the next morning caused general uproar and laughter when she could be heard chatting along with lusty cries of "Bloody bon oeufs" "Bloody bon oeufs".

Merry evenings are spent in the Estaminets where all needs are provided for: fried eggs and chips, very tasty, all kinds of drinks, tea, coffee, beer, wines and spirits a wash and brush up and sometimes a hair cut by the landlord's daughter if required. Strolling in the evening before the general party arrived I find Johnny and Snob, two inseparables of the sanitary squad, having finished their daily task of emptying the latrine pails and digging new latrines, giving a lesson in English conversation to Marie the landlord's daughter and a comely lass. Having had only three pints of beer each so far they have not reached the height of their eloquence. I am greeted and invited to buy some more beer, which I do and then settle down as an observer of two ex-navvies in the role of coaches and Marie as the pupil.

Marie " Where you come monsieur?"
Snob "Cambridge."
Marie "Oh veer-ee good you College?"
Snob "Me no compree,"
Johnny "She wants to know if you are up at college."
Snob "Yes in yer winder blind".
Marie "Monsieur Snob dit oui in yer winder blind? Me spleak good Inglise?"
At this juncture Snob tosses a cigarette end through the open window and Marie says "What you and say in Ong la terre [Angleterre] when you do comme ca?"
Snob "Out the bleeding bird and winder."
Marie "Out bleeding bird and winder, bonne".

Enter a fine young rifleman who greets Marie in good French to which Marie responds. After drinks are served Marie continues "Vous unerstand deux Messier ca make me speak Inglise. Monsieur Snob him come College in Angleterre, him speak veer ee good" and tossing a cork in the direction of the window she says "Out bleeding bird and winder vous think me better?" At this the rifleman bursts into a fit of laughter and when this has subsided asks the inseparables to drink at his expense which they do right heartily.
Together "Well! Here's good `ealth chum and !!!! the Kaiser.
Rifleman "Cheer-ho and how do you find things?"
Snob "Alright here mate."
Rifleman "Yes nice to be back again, we had rather a hot time up at Kemmel this journey, left some jolly fine fellows behind."
Johnny "Oh yer did did yer? Rather hot was it? I wish I was back in Blighty with my

old woman in our little booby hutch, you know I can't see any sense in this ere war can you?"
Rifleman "Well of course you have to look at it from a detached view point you know, honour and glory, love of King and Country and all that sort of thing."
Johnny "Yes I know that's what our officer used to tell us. He used to read books to us and tell us all about battles and esprit-de-corps, I don't know what it means but he's dead now and what's the good of all these things when you are daisy pushing? I told our officer the other day I wanted to give a week's notice he said no, you don't. You're on for duration."

It is very cold and snow is falling and we are marching to a rendezvous where a General is going to inspect us. He arrives in a large motor car and we are disappointed for we have seen no soldiers mounted except transport drivers and we quite expect to see a General dash up on a prancing charger with a mounted body guard. The General says a few words. He is not very cheery. He tells us that there is plenty of hard fighting ahead and that the German troops are not to be despised. We are to keep them busy all the time, to snipe them, strafe them, and put the wind up them at every opportunity. "Remember" he said "when they are strafing you that they are no better off than yourselves and if you bear that in mind and put on a bold front you will get the best of it, at the same time every one of us must be prepared to die if necessary otherwise we might as will not be here." A few more cheery words which on a cold bleak day does us all a power of good and off he goes and so do we, soon warming up as we swing along to some of the old favourite tunes. One Canadian ditty is very popular at this time:

So goodbye boys for ever more
My drinking days are nearly over
Now when I die don't bury me at all
Just pickle my bones in alcohol
Put a bottle of booze at my head and feet
And then I know my soul will sleep.

Then the soldiers' edition of Mademoiselle from Armentières and a few more.

It is Saturday and on Sunday we are to relieve the front line at St. Eloi so to-night we visit the local Estaminets and eat as much food as we can and drink our fill for who knows when we shall get another chance.

St. Eloi remains a small village with a modest amount of new housing. It remembers its place in the conflict with this artillery piece at the crossroads, a flagpole and a plaque with a poem.

After dark we move off and soon become accustomed to familiar surroundings, the constant rise and fall of the Verey lights along the front, the whistle of a shell, the shell burst and then the report of the gun. It is dark as we pass through a sunken road, and apart from the tramp of feet and the rattle of equipment, the intervals between the distant gunfire are very quiet and we seem to be the only people about. A terrific crash, a new sensation of the air suddenly pushing sideways and several simultaneous flashes, and everybody ducks and some throw themselves to the ground but nobody seems to be hurt and we hear a voice in the darkness urging us to get along as quick as we can, it is only one of our batteries firing a salvo on a spit where the enemy are active. Before dawn breaks we are installed in the cellars of a shell shattered village of Voormezeele where we must spend the day in reserve ready for any emergency and prepare to take over the line at night. Dawn breaks and we all start drumming up a handful of charcoal blown into life with a few puffs and one can with practice soon make a mess tin full of cocoa or tea and fry a piece of bacon, if lucky enough to have such a thing. It is delicious.

Our bellies filled, this is one of the joys of life now. Never did it play such a prominent part in our existence. We begin to have a look around but as we have been warned to move with caution we peer through the barricaded front of the cellar gratings.

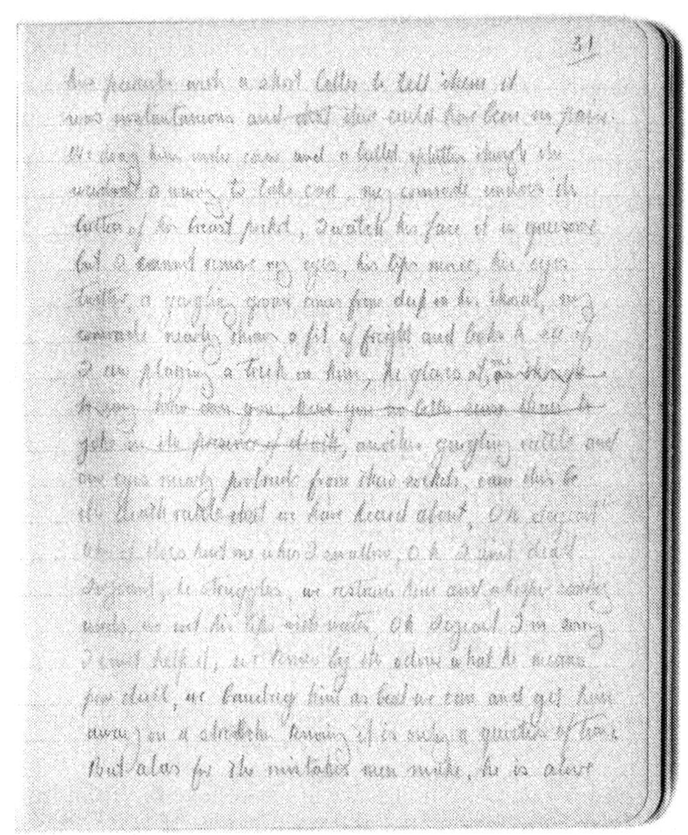

31

[illegible]

But alas for the mistakes men make, he is alive

Opposite is what was once a church, and a graveyard, the stones are broken and uprooted, and large holes partly filled with water gape at one, and look, the splintered side of a coffin with a corpse inside, bones and skulls that seem to laugh in a ghastly fashion lay scattered about. To the right is a mound which overlooks us and everything else, running straight in front round by the church is a road and some distance along its road is a derelict London bus, a strange sight in such a place. The mists clear and the sun breaks through but not a soul can be seen so losing some of our caution we move from house to house searching for souvenirs, but there is not much to be found for doubtless many have been before us. A series of sharp cracks from the directions of the mound and bullets begin to spit around us which causes a general scamper to cover. Who can be firing upon us in this place? Not a sign can be seen of movement anywhere but the intermittent and deliberate crack of a rifle leave no doubt that we are being sniped from some point of vantage. A runner under cover of the back wall of the ruins enters the cellar and tells us that one of our men has a bullet through the brain. So

Images from the graveyard, as taken by Sergeant Stanley.

we set off to search for him. We meet a doctor who tells us that the poor boy is dead, so two men are detailed to dig a hole under cover to bury him. We then proceed up some stairs and looking round the corner of the staircase wall we see a bedroom with one side wall blown away and there lies poor old H with his head among the broken glass of a wardrobe mirror, lips thick, his face pallid like death and a bloody mess oozing from his head. There is no doubt that life has passed from his earthly frame, poor chap. We seem clumsy in his presence, with the cold sun gleaming in his face. Well, we must remove his pay book and personal belongings to send to his parents with a short letter telling them that death was instantaneous and there could have been no pain. We drag him under cover and a bullet splutters through the wardrobe, a warning to take cover. My comrade undoes the button of his breast pocket. I watch his face. It is gruesome but I cannot remove my eyes. His lips move and his eyes roll, a gurgling groan comes from deep in his throat. My comrade nearly throws a fit of fright and looks to see if I am playing a trick on him. He glares at me. Another gurgling rattle and our eyes nearly protrude from their sockets. Can this be the death rattle we have heard about? "Oh! Sergeant. Oh it does hurt me when I swallow, I `aint dead Sergeant". He struggles and moans. We restrain him and whisper soothing words whilst we wet his lips with water. "Oh Sergeant I'm sorry I can't help it". We know by the odour what he means poor devil. We bandage him up as best we can and get him away on a stretcher knowing it is only a question of time. But alas for the mistakes men make. He is alive to-day.

Voormezeele today. The church and tombs are all from later years. The war graves mark the site of a former casualty station.

The day drags on and as dusk approaches we prepare to move forward. We shave, clean rifles, fill our bellies with bully beef and tea ready for the night, the latrine pole in the garden is well filled in the quiet of evening when suddenly hell is let loose, the occupants of the pole scatter like sparrows from a hedgerow and with shirt tails hanging from hastily hoisted slacks dive for the cellars where the dress adjustment is completed. A general scrimmage is taking place to get our equipment, find our rifles and most important to make sure of our rations. A deluge of high explosive shells hits the village like some craft at sea and the noise and effect of concussion is appalling. The air is filled with bursting shrapnel and as darkness draws on the air above appears to be filled with bunches of red hot smouldering rags and above all the rattle of machine gun fire and exploding mines is incessant. An officer dashes up and tells us that the Boche has blown up the front line and broken through. We are to deliver a counter attack at once. Off we go helter skelter up the road round by the church and many fall before we reach the open fields beyond. Here we open out across a field and advance under cover of what was once a hedge, but it is too thick and wired so a gap has to be found and we scramble through, again extending on the other side. We can open fire now but only at the flashes of the Boche as it is too dark to aim properly. We cannot stay here. The Boche has turned machine guns on to us and as they traverse backwards and forwards the bullets sweep to and fro over our heads dealing death to any live object in their path. So on we rush madly, blindly, losing all reason and forgetful of everything, but wildly firing into the flashes that break the dark in the front, forgetful of our bodies. As we struggle through barbed wire we forget our torn and bleeding bodies, stumbling and tripping over the filthy soil of the torn countryside, never before did I realise how a small hollow would afford so much shelter from this devastating death dealing rain of bullets and once one finds refuge in such a spot it requires much moral courage to move, and let me say here if any call this cowardice may they never go through such a terrifying experience. We find an old communication trench half full of water and we tumble in. As we kneel to carry on a rapid fire the water covers our legs and soaks up to the body, but this is nothing now. We do not care. What does anything matter? We can at least get a little shelter from those frightful machine guns, but as though the Boche can read our thoughts the shrapnel barrage creeps slowly nearer and over us striking us from above. A form springs from the trench and runs madly in front of us masking our fire. It is one of our fellows. He has probably lost his reason, no wonder. A chum throwing all caution to the winds catches him and drags him back into the trench. Poor devil, he has a lump of shrapnel shell as large as a hand clinging over his temple like a crab. The blood runs down his face and his shrieks are hideous. The shrapnel cannot be removed so he is bandaged as well as can be and becoming exhausted he pleads for his friend to take him away, but no fighting man can be spared. His pleading is so pitiful that we give way and his friend takes him back, a task that requires a brave heart. The night drags on like some bad nightmare and to our relief things quieten a little. We are only a handful now isolated it seems from the world and everything that has been before. We get in touch with some scattered troops on our left and advance into a village where hard house to house fighting is taking place. We are now too weak to do much but act on the defensive until reinforcements arrive. These arrive early in the morning and after a sharp and bloody struggle retake the line and consolidate. The stragglers are gathered together under NCOs and spare officers, and begin a weary trek back to reserve billets, for dawn is beginning to break and we must not be caught in the open in daylight or few will be left to tell the tale. The fates are kind to us this morning for a heavy mist hangs over the ground. What a sight one meets, what a collection of bloody, weary, torn and mutilated demented so-called humanity, little more than hunted beasts, staring frightful eyes, men with shattered limbs being assisted by faithful comrades, some crawling on hands and knees craving for succour, and those brave fellows that we used to refer to as "poultice wallahs", the gallant R.A.M.C. risking their lives all the time, tending the wounded and working like Trojans to give relief to suffering, an improvised dressing station where the doctors have been at work throughout the night at their ghastly task, a row of stiff bodies outside some who will not answer the roll call. I try to collect my thoughts I wonder what my mother is doing now and my brother but I lose the trend. A tune persists in running through my mind

"The bells of Hell went ting-a-ling-a-ling
For you but not for me"

Where are Tom and Ted and Bert and -

"Oh death where is thy sting-a-ling-a-ling".

I wonder if our Officer has been hit.

"O grave thy victory."

I wonder who was the occupant I had seen through the side of the coffin in the churchyard at Voormezeele and what it was like in life, and those laughing skulls who did they belong to.

"The Bells of Hell wait ..."

Up early in the morning, ready to move off with full kit. We have heard a rumour that we are to relieve the French in front of Ypres and all is agog with excitement. We are to relieve the French troops defending "Ypres". Wipers. That name that had been on every tongue for months, what would it be like, how should we find it? But for the moment we are fully occupied humping a full pack over the metalled roads, and to make things a trifle more uncomfortable there is a fairly general attack of diarrhoea due to the news that we are off to a hot quarter or it may be due to over filling our stomachs whilst we had the chance. Anyway, it is a pretty rotten business marching with a full kit with all your buttons undone ready for an emergency, a sudden dash from the ranks and then a double to get back to your place, but this does not go on for long and we soon get going again in anticipation of what lies in front.

The great medieval cloth hall that we see in Ypres today was rebuilt after the conflict. The scaffolding seen by Sergeant Stanley would prove to be of little help in the course of three great battles fought in the Ypres area and the constant shelling of the town.

Tramp tramp, left right, left right on through Vlamertinghe, next stop Ypres. We meet a few more troops now but mostly details arranging depots for the Division and some of them tell us that we are entering Ypres. We see civilians, women and children, a water tower in the distance, and apart from a few shattered houses, not many signs of war. The shops gaily exhibit their wares and the girls greet us as we march along. As we enter the main square we see on our left the Cloth Hall surrounded by scaffolding, giving the appearance from outside of an old building being renovated but upon examination the interior proved to be a mass of disordered debris. We are detailed to find billets for the night and we spent the evening looking around searching for souvenirs and of course a visit to the Estaminets. Food in these places is not plentiful here so we have to arrange a feast with army rations and any oddments we can buy. A party of about six of us find a seed merchant's shop just inside the Menin Gate. Of course the house has been struck by a shell and the tenants have left everything in disorder. We find one of those comfortable French box spring mattresses and draw lots who shall share it. I am one of the lucky four. We next toss up to decide who shall cook the feast, I again am lucky for it falls to the lot of a Corporal and after we all have a good scrounge around, a right royal feast it is. Just opposite the billet is an enormous shell crater almost big enough to put a house in, and another in the square. Upon enquiring we are told that they were caused by shells from a new German gun of enormous caliber and it speaks well for the German gunners that the one outside our billet is within a few yards of the stone bridge over the canal, which it would have completely demolished. Coming from the Menin Gate towards the Square we turn up a side turning to the left and in a courtyard we find a latrine and sit to enjoy ourselves for next to eating and drinking this is one of the things that really gives enjoyment now that we are cut off from the convivialities. So having settled comfortably in a row, we discuss the latest rumours, pretty girls we have known or seen and general tit-bits of gossip with a few smutty yarns for those who appreciate them. When a particularly

Today's Menin gate from outside the city walls. Every night the last post continues to be sounded here to remember those who died at Ypres.

good story is told it meets with applause from the rear and all continue to beat the others in quantity or quality. We have grown accustomed by habit to this form of entertainment by now and are not at all abashed, but when a nun appears in her familiar garb all and sundry are stricken dumb and do not know where to hide their faces. The good lady is least embarrassed of all and with averted face goes her way. Probably close contact with suffering humanity in this stricken area had purged her mind of all but innocence. Anyway it is a more sober party that hoists their slacks and go their way. We learned afterwards that these good folk move freely and without fear among the troops watching over their flock and doing what good they can.

Good Friday March 1915

Between 17th March and 26th May 1915 the Regiment were at the front line at Ypres.

Today the road east from Ypres runs straight as ever but the steady flow of cars replaces the tramp of boots.

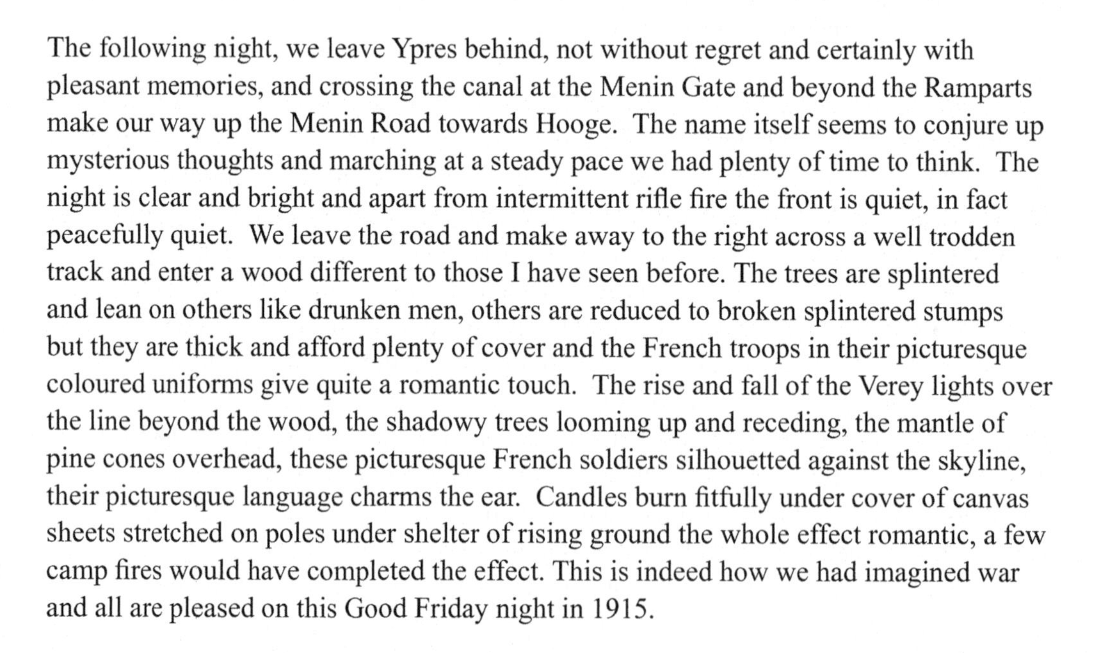

The following night, we leave Ypres behind, not without regret and certainly with pleasant memories, and crossing the canal at the Menin Gate and beyond the Ramparts make our way up the Menin Road towards Hooge. The name itself seems to conjure up mysterious thoughts and marching at a steady pace we had plenty of time to think. The night is clear and bright and apart from intermittent rifle fire the front is quiet, in fact peacefully quiet. We leave the road and make away to the right across a well trodden track and enter a wood different to those I have seen before. The trees are splintered and lean on others like drunken men, others are reduced to broken splintered stumps but they are thick and afford plenty of cover and the French troops in their picturesque coloured uniforms give quite a romantic touch. The rise and fall of the Verey lights over the line beyond the wood, the shadowy trees looming up and receding, the mantle of pine cones overhead, these picturesque French soldiers silhouetted against the skyline, their picturesque language charms the ear. Candles burn fitfully under cover of canvas sheets stretched on poles under shelter of rising ground the whole effect romantic, a few camp fires would have completed the effect. This is indeed how we had imagined war and all are pleased on this Good Friday night in 1915.

A guide directs us across some open ground between two small woods then up a trench into the heart of a thick wood and we are in the front line. We are surprised for we thought we should pass through some reserves but if there were any they must have been in the woods at the rear. All is excitement and bustle as we pass along the trench, shaking hands and being embraced by the French soldiers who give us a most enthusiastic welcome and in exchanging cigarettes we found afterwards that they had the best of the deal. For the moment we all seem to forget that the Boche exist so as best we can we ask where the Boche trenches are and noticing rabbit wire stretched across poles on top of the parapet we are curious to know what it is for. It is very soon apparent. One of our Allies puts up a Verey light and observing through a steel loophole in the sandbags the Boche parapet can be plainly seen within good throwing distance but with one comforting factor, the ground between generally known as No Man's Land is such a mass of splintered jagged timber, the remains of what once were trees and barbed wire that it is well nigh impassable. Our allies depart and sentries are posted whilst the remainder settle down for a little rest in improvised shelters made by cutting a shelf into the back of the trench, laying poles across the top and covering them with branches, old waterproof sheets and sandbags. In these shelters it is possible to snatch a few hours sleep and make tea or cocoa. The night passes uneventfully and at dawn everyone begins to take stock of the surroundings, this being our first experience of the front line. Owing to the very close proximity of the enemy at this point all observation is carried out with periscopes and through these, the two lines can be seen zigzagging away to the right and out of the wood where they were further apart. To our surprise trails of smoke can be seen rising from different points along the enemy trenches where no doubt the Hun is busy preparing his breakfast and it did not take our fellows long to follow their example. After breakfast signs of activity can be observed opposite. Our attention is attracted by a spade waving above the parapet but this is treated with caution for several of our fellows already have small wounds through looking through the steel loopholes so the dangerous ones are carefully avoided and only those which apparently are unobserved are used. There is great excitement when the periscope man reported a notice being put along the parapet where the spade has been waving and hardly believing his eyes he hands the periscope over to several others and there sure enough is a roughly scrawled "Happy Easter". The German intelligence has the sense of humour to inform us in two words that English troops have relieved the French during the previous night. In spite of their good wishes they keep up a continuous sniping fire with a bomb at intervals. It can now be seen why the rabbit wire is stretched upright above the parapet. Having no other means of retaliation we selected several good points of vantage and commenced to snipe, choosing loopholes opposite the periscope man sporting hits and misses. This, however causes our neighbours little embarrassment for after a time our old friend the spade begins to give signals in our own range method of hits and misses. They apparently have a strong sense of humour, but it is no joke and rather spoils the fun when a very large Sergeant who is recording for me suddenly lurched back against the back of the trench and throws up his hands to his to face which is covered with blood. A German bullet has struck the top plate mirror of the periscope, deflected down the box, shattered the bottom plate glass mirror, projecting the splintered glass onto my friend's face and into his eyes, momentarily blinding him.

Easter Sunday 1915

It rained hard all night and it is a dispirited muddy party that sees the dawn break this Easter Sunday morning, soaked to the skin with very little chance of getting dry again, numbed by the intense cold and every time we move from our high spot to another it means splashing about through water over the ankles for there are no duck boards here. A machine gun opens up from some concealed spot opposite and deftly cuts the supporting poles thus letting down the rabbit wire. This is followed by a shower of bombs which cause a helter skelter this way and that, round a traverse, back again, a rush here and a rush there until we manage to shore up some fresh poles. We are then treated to a little rifle grenade practice and these having a high trajectory like a howitzer shell are landed straight into the trench from above, but a little experience and a sharp lookout and one can see them take the time in mid air ready for the drop and it does not take long to get round the nearest traverse.

This is apparently only the opening chapter for then the guns open up, the shells seem to whistle, moan and roar just over the parapet bursting some distance in the rear, probably in the woods where reserves might be quartered. So long as they keep a safe distance we need not worry. They slowly but surely creep nearer and nearer, the roar and the burst are all mixed up. Trees crash to the ground, some falling across the trench, trying it seems to crush us. The noise is deafening. The effect of concussion gives a pain in the eardrums and the trench crumbles and weak spots fall in. Nearer and nearer creeps this terrible inferno which can only end in death. May it come quick and mercifully. Some poor wretch has the side of his skull blown away and it is obvious that nothing can be done for him. Oh the horror of it all. Why does it take so long for a man to die? We are trapped like rats, we cannot go forward, the way is barred and even if we could machine guns and rifles are waiting to mow us down like a scythe. We cannot go right or left, we cannot go back, we can only wait numbed and stupefied. Why can't our guns reply? Then perhaps the Hun would give us a respite, but in spite of the din it is quite obvious which way all the shells are coming.

Just when it seems that human endurance can stand no more the shelling stops as suddenly as it had started and our courage restored with the thought that some of us can still live on a little longer we are set to repairing the damage, and dealing with the wounded who cannot be got away until darkness falls. We ask one artillery observer why our guns do not reply. Our shells are rationed and can only be used if the enemy breaks through. Rather cheerful news this but facts speak for themselves and it doesn't require much intelligence to know who has the guns and shells. Anyway, if it is our side it must be silent ones. Our rifles are of the old long type with a short wooden hand guard and after a short spell of rapid fire they burn the hands unless used with care, the bolt jambs and has to be forced open with an entrenching tool handle. We have two old Maxim guns, bombs are very crude. They seem to be made from old jam tins and the fuses cut off to the required number of inches and ignited with a fusee match - a very crude affair altogether.

Night again and we are relieved. We move back to a sunken wood and steal a few snatches of fitful sleep in what are for some misguided reason called dugouts. They afford practically no protection from the invisible peril that fills the air and still less shelter from the incessant rain. During the day we work hard improving things for the benefit no doubt of the people who follow us. At night fatigue parties are detailed to

A fascinating photograph, labelled by Sergeant Stanley 'A hopeless dawn'. Whether he took it with the intent of conveying some sense of gloom at that time or whether he looked at it some time later and felt the caption appropriate, we can't know.

carry necessaries between the dumps in the rear and the front line trenches. After dark the country just behind the line is like giant ant heaps with hosts of sweating, swearing, cursing frenzied human beings stumbling in the darkness with their varied burdens - boxes of ammunition, sandbags full of rations, timber for the tunnellers, jars and tins of horrible chlorinated water which are usually dumped on route for one would rather drink the water from shell holes or land drains that run into the trenches and risk enteric or dysentery, than drink this beastly chlorinated concoction which leaves a horrid twang in the mouth and spoils the flavour of tea or cocoa, jars of rum intimately referred to affectionately as S.R.D. This is a job much coveted, for a few pals can conveniently stumble in a shell hole, fill their water bottles with this comforting spirit, knock the bottom from the jar and produce the handle and part of the jar as evidence that they had fallen and broken it. Engineers' stores have to be carried, long poles with a wooden cross at each end, the whole covered with barbed wire and called knife rests. These are used as barricades where stakes and wire cannot be erected. At one dump called White Horse Dump half a horse reposes in the branches of a tree and the bleaching effect of the elements causes it to show up almost white, hence the name. A horrible smell hangs around this spot, the smell of dead horses, distinct from the smell of dead men, in spite of the application of chloride of lime for it is a long job to bury a dead horse, and we have already had the experience of having to cut a trench through a spot where some have been buried and what is worse to live there for some days.

A few days of this gruelling work and we all began to wish ourselves back in the front line again and our wish is soon gratified for in the afternoon we take over number 2 trench from the Irish. This is away to the right in the direction of Hill 60. The trenches are about 100 yards apart, there are no trees, and both trenches are on level ground almost like a table formed by the high ground. There is no cover here and very little wire. A road runs diagonally between the opposing lines and has probably been the scene of hard fighting for dead Germans still hang on the barbed wire and

A concrete machine gun emplacement on Hill 60 today. The area continues to give just an inkling of how it was nearly a century ago, with various memorials and a panoramic photograph which shows bayonets poking up above the parapets.

strew the ground in front, the trench is strung and well sandbagged. There are no loopholes and all firing is done from the fire step upon which we stand. This is a new experience for the head and shoulders are exposed above the parapet. The Irish at this point seem to have the enemy well subdued and just to prove their superiority before they depart we all man the parapet and open up a terrific burst of rapid fire into and just above the enemy parapet, we then all fix bayonets and show them above the parapet, this apparently being an Irish way of putting fear into the enemy who we were told imagine crouching in the trenches opposite, expecting the worst to happen, this incident has a wonderful tonic effect upon us novices.

Through a hole in the parapet a sap runs into No Man's Land through the wire a distance of about 30 yards which has to be manned by two men from dusk to dawn and we are told to pay particular attention to this listening post as the previous night two men mysteriously disappeared and had not returned. Over to the left the line is not continuous but connected by a loop, the intervening space being wired and covered by a machine gun post. To the left of the listening post just outside the wire lay two bodies which look like German Officers. They have fine helmets and partly under their bodies can be observed leather wallets and an argument takes place as to whether they contain revolvers, field glasses, or maybe anything. Anyhow, we determine that when it gets properly dark we will investigate and get some souvenirs. They must have been there sometime for they show signs of exposure, the skin stretched across the cheekbones is black giving the appearance of black skulls, the tunic about the waistline appears eaten away. There is no chance to get any rest here for owing to its exposed position we must all be ready at the least sign to repel a raid. Volunteers are called for in pairs to take two hour shifts in the listening post and all are willing with the exception of two. One poor devil must be excused for whilst carrying a lot of ammunition a shell passed between him and the fellow on the other side of the box in such close proximity that it threw them both to the ground. The other fellow had to be sent back a chattering, gibbering, shell shocked wreck, but this fellow hangs on with a silent dogged determination and although he is not much use he will see it through with the rest of us, and so it came about that one of these splendid young boys with us, boys who should still be at school, offered to take a double shift. This meets with all round approval but when another boy offers to do the other man's share, they would not listen, and the shirker a fine young athlete much given to boasting when danger was past had a rough experience at the hands of lads who had been the victims of his bullying ways in England and behind the lines for he had a stripe. You may wonder why the Officers seem to play no part in this particular adventure. I suppose they are here alright directing operations and passing orders on to us but I only have a recollection of meeting one during this time and the meeting was not cordial for he was trying to pass in a narrow muddy trench and because my feet were embedded in the mud and it was no easy job to move quickly he struck me in the back with a wooden stave like a scouts pole and if ever I have felt the lust to murder it was then, but he got his reward later, perish the thought, there were all too few of them and they were terribly overworked, after all they were the same flesh and blood as ourselves. Eager eyes peer through the darkness in the direction of the two bodies in front like eagles waiting to devour their prey, each hoping to claim some souvenir, until when all is quiet, two youngsters slip through the hole in the parapet and up the listening post sap, through our wire then crawl towards their prize. They are soon back struggling through the hole in the parapet, properly scared and after a good deal of leg pulling they swear they saw the bodies move. Two more have a try and tell the same tale so we put up a light and give a burst of rapid fire but they are still there. This is rather disconcerting to the listening post reliefs who are well in front of this point, especially after the uncanny experience of our predecessors and nothing upsets the nerves more than mystery especially when you may find a knife between your ribs at any moment. Nobody seems keen on investigating further after this and so the souvenirs are not claimed and the interminable night passes on wings of lead and we approach another cold relentless dawn, merely another dawn when spirits ebb low and the very marrow in one's bones seems to freeze, a gnawing emptiness at the pit of the stomach, feet that have lost feeling, eyes that ache and smart through peering into the darkness throughout the night, but this feeling soon passes and a restless feeling springs into life. As the dawn breaks, we commence sniping and there is plenty of opportunity here but as the light increases and as it becomes too risky we set to drumming up something hot to drink and a snack to eat. Some of the youngsters still continue to snipe in spite of the advice of older men, and this leads to a good deal of swearing for some of the return shots skim the parapet and sprinkle the soil into the mess tins of tea and it is too precious to waste it is not improved in flavour. One mere boy begs for just one more shot, he fires, he is elated at the result of his shot, his trigger finger points along the trigger guard parallel with the barrel, he falls back off the fire step and like some puppy that has been trodden on he yelps, "I got it, I got it". His trigger finger is cleaved apart as with a knife, a very narrow shave but nevertheless a Blighty wound envied by all. Letters arrive from home. I get a photo of a pretty girl whose young brother is in my Platoon and I have promised to look after him. What a delusion, for here we all take the same chance and he being smaller than myself probably stands the better chance for there is not so much to get hit. He looks wistfully towards me, I believe he would follow me into hell itself. He seems just a small frail girl himself and I shall not let him down. Why I wonder should this boy be involved in this wicked murderous game. If he survives he can never forget and when I think of that big fellow for whom he offered to do listening post duty I go all hot. Poor old Punch has a letter from his mother, some poor mother who probably mourns him still. He can neither read nor write. I read it to him and write a reply. He is a rough diamond with a heart of gold and when there is any dirty work about he is there. He prowls around in No Man's Land at night and brings back all kinds of odds and ends and all kinds of queer yarns of what old Von

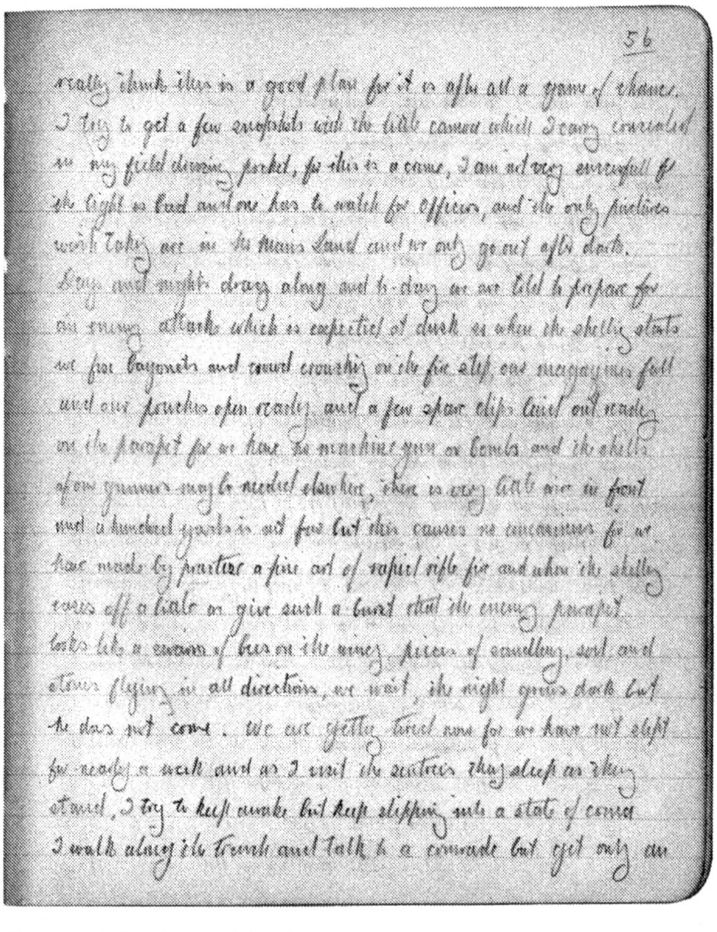
56
really think this is a good plan for it is after all a game of chance.
I try to get a few snapshots with the little camera which I carry concealed
in my field dressing pocket, for this is a crime, I am not very successfull for
the light is bad and one has to watch for officers, and the only pictures
worth taking are in No Mans Land and we only go out after dark.
Days and nights drag along and to-day we are told to prepare for
an enemy attack which is expected at dusk so when the shelling starts
we fix bayonets and crawl crouching on the fire step our magazines full
and our pouches open ready and a few spare clips laid out ready
on the parapet for we have no machine guns or bombs and the shells
of our gunners may be needed elsewhere, there is very little wire in front
and a hundred yards is not far but this causes no uneasiness for we
have made by practice a fine art of rapid rifle fire and when the shelling
eases off a little we give such a burst that the enemy parapet
looks like a swarm of bees on the wing, pieces of sandbag, soil and
stones flying in all directions, we wait, the night grows dark but
he does not come. We are getting tired now for we have not slept
for nearly a week and as I visit the sentries they sleep as they
stand, I try to keep awake but keep slipping into a state of coma
I walk along the trench and talk to a comrade but get only an

Sergeant Stanley evidently thought that recording friends and events for posterity was worth the risk of carrying the camera; there was relatively little use of personal cameras at that time anyway, so his doing this is all the more remarkable.

Cluck is doing over yonder. He is quite harmless and keeps us well supplied with trench stores and timber to make shelters and fires. "Spare Me" has no mail so he shares the others. He is bad on his feet and by his gait or shuffle and his nickname he is well known to the neighbouring troops. He has a reputation for scrounging and has a flair for finding a ration dump or a jar of rum and many an officer and the troops a bit extra through the machination of "Spare Me". "Boko" is chuckling over his letter in his droll way. He never hurries, in fact he has never been known to run even in the hottest corner. He just takes his time and really I think it is a good plan for after all it is a game of chance. I try to get a few snapshots with the little camera I carry concealed in my field dressing pocket, for this is a crime. I am not very successful for the light is bad and one has to watch for officers and the only pictures worth taking are in No Man's Land and we only go out after dark. Days and nights drag along and today we are told to prepare for an enemy attack which is expected at dusk, so when the shelling starts we fix bayonets and crawl crouching on the firestep our magazines full and our pouches open ready and a few spare clips laid out ready on the parapet for we have no machine guns or bombs and the shells of our gunners may be needed elsewhere. There is very little wire in front and a hundred yards is not far but this causes no uneasiness for we have made by practice a fine art of rapid rifle fire and when the shelling eases off a little we give such a burst that the enemy parapet looks like a swarm of bees on the wing, pieces of sandbag, soil and stones flying in all directions. We wait. The night grows dark but he does not come.

We are getting tired for we have not slept for nearly a week and as I visit the sentries they sleep as they stand. I try to keep awake but keep slipping into a state of coma. I walk along the trench and talk to a comrade but only get an incoherent reply. He is also in a state of coma. I try to reason with him and remind him of the penalty of sleeping on sentry go on active service. I know what I am saying quite clearly as one does in a dream but cannot rouse myself. I try to shout but my voice has no sound. A pain in my neck and a weight pressing on my head I throw forward both hands to remove this thing that oppresses me. My loaded rifle clatters from my grasp to the bottom of the trench and I find that my oppressor is none other than the side of the trench where with my head resting I have fallen asleep. We must fight against this new terror. One fellow has a mouth organ. He plays and we sing. "Spare Me" scrounges a jar of rum and we still have some tea and sugar and plenty of water and charcoal. We are fortunate for water

Three photographs from those taken by Sergeant Stanley and one of the war memorial at Poperinge today.

A cow wandering up to the bivouac warrants a photo and relaxing times fishing at a canal and at the river.

The town of Poperinge was for most of the war a safe distance behind the front line and held happy memories for Sergeant Stanley (p. 62). Sadly one of the few places recalled there today is the spot where a number of deserters were shot during the course of the war.

for our trench cuts through a land drain and by filling the opening with charcoal we get a plentiful supply of sweet water. It is time to change the listening post sentries. One sentry is here and reminds me he is ready. The other, "the young athlete" who shirked before cannot be found. After a search he is found crouching in the loop trench some distance to the rear and says he will not return, the fool. If an Officer should come along it will mean a court martial and I shall have to give evidence and sure enough he will face a firing squad and the risk at no time during the war was greater than now. I go alone and find him for there is no need to make his degradation greater. He shrinks from me. I command him to return. I threaten to shoot him and am tempted to pull

A couple more photographs from about this time; no further information on the left hand picture and a sergeant with two puppies on his lap in the right hand picture.

the trigger but this carries no fear. I reason with him to play the game and be a man, to master this fear that grips him. I tell him quite truthfully of my own fear which I dare not let my comrades know of. Sinking on his knees as in supplication he pleads for relief and the tears roll down his cheeks. "I cannot. I will not go out there again. Shoot me if you will, send me back under arrest, do what you like. I cannot. I cannot." As I crouch out there and peer into the darkness and see all those dead bodies beckoning to me, leering at me, those glaring eyes that seem to pierce through me, the aggressive eyes of corpse rats that will attack me next. It is no use as I coax him back and tell the other fellows he is unwell and another fellow does his bit. (This soldier wins distinction for gallantry later.) I shall not report him. I know what this fear is. We all know it at some time or another but some conceal it better than others. The next reliefs are given a good dose of rum and pushed through the hole in the parapet but they soon return. A shudder runs through my spine as this thing has happened again as it did with our predecessors. What can be the meaning of it? What is this mystery, for no movement has been observed from the trench. Well it must be investigated and I would it fell to the lot of anyone but me. My young friend by my side without the necessity of calling for a volunteer and we commenced our eerie crawl up this mysterious gap. Just through our wire my hair nearly pushes my cap off as a loud squealing commenced. Two big corpse rats are having an encounter in and out of the side of one of the dead Germans. This may be the explanation of the report that these corpses had been seen to move. It seemed ages before we reached the sap head and in the darkness two forms could be seen huddled close together. With nerves on edge and eyes and ears straining for any sound or movement and bayonets ready to thrust we waited and simultaneously we let out a hysterical laugh for we both recognize the snoring of one of the sentries. The poor devils are fast asleep. On this day an inhuman military code is cheated of three victims but it is only a respite for the crime of war claimed two of them later.

Two days respite back in Ypres, it is different now. The civilians have gone and the nuns, the Estaminets are closed and shell craters are everywhere. Sack, rot, ruin, desolation. Hungry dogs prowl around in packs and what once were happy well-tended homes now litter the streets. So this is this glorious thing called war, the result of ages of so called civilization and culture. What has the Church been doing to allow this thing? These wooden crosses that litter this once fertile countryside, those once healthy smiling men that lay now beneath the soil, some not even accorded this decency, the people that mourn, thank God they do not know those devilish Germans who have brought this thing upon us, but they too have people that mourn but what could one do? We have ceased to be human beings now. We are just cogs in this colossal war machine. If we refuse to be parties to this thing we shall be shot as traitors. If we desist from killing the enemy he will kill us. We have even sunk so low that we will raid our comrades ration dumps if opportunity offers and fill our bellies, not caring whether they go hungry or not for we are cunning as the lower animals and resort to any subterfuge to continue living. We were not disappointed because we haven't the courage to rob dead men of their material trinkets. The penalty of being caught looting is death but we are undeterred for everybody is doing it and what is the good of acquiring loot for sooner or later death will claim us. It passes through the ranks when least expected and takes its toll indiscriminately respecting neither rank nor creed. Some answer the call with a smile, some with a curse, some go quietly and others struggle against it but none come back. So we will loot. We find some clean refined underwear in a deserted chateaux outside the ramparts. We undress and cast off our lousy underwear and don the new and oh what a comfort to be free from lice, this awful continuous irritation until one could scratch oneself to pieces. Some wine is produced and we sit in our newly acquired underwear and proceed to delouse our tunics and trousers. This is a long job and must be done thoroughly and even as they breed so quickly that after the most careful search one is soon alive again. An old tin lid with a lighted candle underneath is the crematorium and into this the ones that show fight are thrust and soon frizzle. The ones that have not yet reached this stage are nipped between the two thumbnails and signal their departure by a distinct snap. There are some nice paintings on the walls. I make my choice. I don't know of what use a painting will be to me in the front line but cannot overcome this feeling of greed, this greed to acquire, if only for a short time. My comrades find some other valuables and we find some francs with which we can gamble at night and so we prepare to depart when half through a basement window an officer stands looking at me. It is too late to retreat so I salute and spring to attention. To my surprise and relief he bids me good afternoon and asks if this is my billet. I reply no but there are some things of interest to be seen inside whereupon he asks me if he may look around. I accede to his request and with an air of authority I put my head through the open window and command my scared comrades to stand aside to let an Officer pass. He passes and so do we and vanish as quickly as our legs will carry us. We must be more cautious. It is grand to feel clean and free from those tormenting lice. To once again feel one's feet, to know that one has feet dry and warm, to stride along and fill the lungs, to raise the head without fear of some sniper's eye seeing it, to live above ground like men and not to crawl about like vermin in mud and blood and the filthy smells that must be when large numbers of men live under trench conditions and to be able to sleep, a wonderful feeling that even the shells and the incessant rattle of transport cannot disturb, but all good things come to an end and we are off again to take over Trench 14 in front of Sanctuary Wood, another trench among the splintered woodland with Fritz just across the road with very little chance of making each other's acquaintance unless he detonates a mine gallery beneath us and then if we are fortunate it will all be over quickly and we shall not know much about it. This is quite a good trench with duckboards which lift our feet from the water and adds greatly to the sense of comfort. A straight trench runs parallel with the fire trench . "Spare Me" reports that he has located the Officers' dugout and also the servants' where the Officers' food is cooked and prepared. This is good tiding for we shall probably get some luxury. The only thing it seems possible to scrounge is a fairly large tin of something so a plot is hatched. "Spare Me" puts a little soil in his empty sandbag and sets off behind the fatigue party. As he passes the Officers' dugout the tin accidentally falls into the sandbag, which is then filled with soil and built into the parapet with the others and so the work continues. A hue and cry goes up. The Officers have lost a large tin of preserved strawberries. Wherever can they have gone, runners, N.C.O.s, and even Officers make a search but the mystery is unsolved until the following night when we have the best feed of fruit since we left England. Our little shelter is quite comfortable and homely and the earth floor is even beginning to crack with the warmth. It is about six feet long, four feet deep and four feet high. A comrade is lying full length along the back trying to write a letter by the light of flickering candle, another sits at one end with his feet hanging outside and curses when some awkward mother's son kicks them in passing along the trench. An old corned beef tin full of holes glows brightly as it is fed from time to time with a few pieces of charcoal, a mess tin full of water begins to boil and we are looking forward to a hot drink of café-au-lait. My comrade jealously guards the boiling water as I open the tin. The fire and the mess tin seem to be playing tricks or is it the effect of the flickering candle. It appears as if some living thing shudders in the soil under the fire. Surely I am not getting the rats. The comrade stops writing and looks at the curious effect. He then looks at me. None of us voice any opinion but we all think there is something funny. Anyway we will make sure of one coffee and investigate later. We move the fire and feel the earth. It is soft like a balloon. We scrape the soil away and come upon a blanket and then a brown waterproof sheet, and then a French tunic. We cover it up, we place the soil back, we are silent. We are sharing the grave of a French Poiler[3], but we will not move. He will not mind for he also was a soldier and thought the things we think and did the things we do, three alive here in this grave and one departed and but for the providence of fate we may all share it in the same state before dawn.

The troops on our right take Hill 60 after a bloody slaughter and are rewarded by being blown back again in the morning. One of our Companies in reserve is sent to counter attack with other troops but our Company is caught in the open and almost annihilated leaving us without support. It is Sunday again and we know this by the Strafe. We are issued with extra iron rations and sling bandoliers of ammunition all over our anatomy. It is wonderful the number of projections we find and we look like a lot of Christmas trees all dressed up. It is difficult to walk and goodness knows how we shall run and use the bayonet as we have been taught. It seems to me that if we fall or lay down, the night will not allow us to rise again. We stand to and at six o'clock an aeroplane will give a signal and over we go and with good luck we shall break through and it will all be over in a few weeks, so we are told, but goodness knows how we are expected to get over here. Perhaps we shall move along out of the wood into the open country beyond. A feeling of suspense pervades everything and it seems that the time will never come to get going when we hear the drone of aircraft which gives a smoke signal and we commence rapid fire. The guns open up like drums. The whole earth as far as the vision reaches seems to open and crash and flash and rock. Where once clusters of trees hid the view is now barren open country; hills are changed to valleys. The whole landscape has changed in a few minutes. We are dazed and deafened. We can even see the enemy manhandling field guns into position behind his line but too far away to have much effect with rifle fire and our guns seem to be fully occupied away on the right of Hill 60 and Mount Kemmell. If only we had a few batteries of 75s or the 18 pounders, what slaughter could be done. Darkness covers everything and it is apparent that we shall not go over tonight. The alarm is sounded and everybody stands to. The trenches glow redly against the black sky as though on fire. We have seen before the isolated glow of trench fires but nothing quite like this before so we give a burst of rapid fire just to let them know that we are ready and waiting if they care to try any tricks, when to our surprise a shower of flaming bushes are thrown well out into No Man's Land and we soon realize what the game is for a fresh wind is blowing across our trench and the small dry timber on top of the tangled mass soon takes up the flames which quickly run across and make our trench an inferno. The smoke, the heat and the sparks blind and burn and we are helpless to return the fire until a retreat has to be made into the communicating trench. During this time the enemy pours a murderous fire into our parapet and as the fire burns the canvas from the sandbags, the soil runs out and the machine guns played havoc. After the first blaze up of the small dry timber the fire burns more slowly and we are able to get back to the trench and with old tins full of water the smouldering sandbags are damped out and bad spots repaired but we are still in a sorry plight. Just before dawn when our position is becoming intolerable a cheer goes up as the wind begins to veer round and carry the flames back onto the enemy parapet and how we cheer and fire. At intervals old pails could be seen projecting water over the enemy parapet and every time this happens a shower of bullets strike the pails and tears down the breastwork. The devils, so they would burn us alive. This is not war but why did we not think of it first. I remember a dark hint dropped by an old sweat at St. Eloi. I get some wire cutters and cut the ends off a clip of bullets and throw the pieces well into No Man's Land for I know full well the penalty if I am caught by my own Officers or the Germans. I aim at a spot where the flames are licking the breastwork and blaze away and am rewarded by seeing the breastwork vanish as if some fiend were at work with invisible spade. Demoniacally I repeat the process until exhausted and then I begin to have pangs of remorse. I have seen some terrible wounds caused by these things, but it wasn't human to try and burn us alive. My honour is deserting me and I haven't seen much glory. We are relieved by another Company and move into close support in the woods just behind the line managing to steal a few hours sleep during the day and digging trenches at night under cover of darkness, but we would rather be back in the front line for in support the shelling is continuous now and aircraft is becoming more active so that we cannot light fires, the fumes given off by the bursting shells hang about in the woods, making the eyes and nostrils smart and causing a pain in the lungs. The stretcher bearers tell us strange stories of men dying in agony, at the dressing stations, without wounds, and it is hinted that the shells contain poison gas against which we have no protection. Our Lieut. is a medical student and he thinks he detects chlorine gas and suggests that we make some pads of fibrous soil wrapped in a handkerchief and soaked in our own urine and if it gets worse to clamp these pads over the mouth and nostrils. These pads we hang on our equipment ready for emergency and when we urinate we see that the pads are well-soaked and kept moist.

It is a strange thought that we struggling, suffering mortals cut off from civilization, surrounded by an impenetrable barrier from which there seems no escape, are yet so close to nature which persists like some of us in surviving, for here are hawthorns and almonds in spite of being splintered, torn and burned throwing out their fragrant colourful blooms, tops of trees severed from their roots, but still bursting into blossom, sweet smelling violets which take us back to happier times in fragrant woods at this time of year. A hare lies in a hole in a field outside the wood but it pays for its folly for we soon snipe it and hand it over to the cook. It is night again and the ration party sets off to the rear to carry up rations, stores and ammunition and each time this process becomes more nerve-racking for the shelling and machine gun is continuous, the shell craters and shattered trees more numerous and in a condition far from fit the load seems heavier. In trying to jump a stream in the dark with a loaded sandbag I land in a heap almost on top of a comrade in front who curses and swears that I have trodden on his heel and as he limps along cursing and grumbling I curse him in return. We get back safely and in a shelter we light a candle to investigate his trouble, but he creates such a fuss that we cannot remove his boot and for a good reason, for a spent bullet has penetrated his boot and is fast embedded in his heel. We jerk it out with some pliers, treat him with iodine and send him back - another lucky blighty.

We take our trench No 13, just our luck. I am not superstitious as a rule, but funny things happen now. The shelling increases in intensity, but most of them seem to travel in the direction of Ypres. The large ones seem to pass a never ending stream like the roar on the underground railway, others seem to travel on like a sudden gust of wind, others moan on a rising note which end in a bump; others scream and hurtle as though they have lost their equilibrium and do not know where to settle, and the small ones suddenly seem to leap from nowhere and fly at one's head with a terrifying whiz bang-bang.

The enemy have been relieved by fresh troops who are more aggressive; they snipe all the time and keep bumping trench mortars over, big things like barrels which give off thick clouds of black smoke, wreck the trench, and scatter death-dealing showers of old razor blades, nails, and all kinds of odds and ends. The French fighting has moved round to the left by Polygon Wood across the Menin Road. We are told that the French have coloured troops there, but our real knowledge is confined to a few hundred yards where we happen to be; the rest of the world is a blank, the isolation is complete. The line is thinly held and with no supports. Ypres can be seen a few miles behind us glowing like a huge bonfire night after night, the Verey lights are all round us - they even seem to be behind us. No news arrives and worse still no rations. We retrieve some tins of bully beef that we have thrown into "“No Man's Land" and some concrete biscuits that we had used for fuel when charcoal ran short. After a time these stick in the gullet and refuse to be swallowed, and the salt of the bully beef parches the tongue so that we drink ravenously of doubtful water. Have we been deceived, misled, betrayed? If only we knew what was happening. If only something could be done. In any case we have plenty of cartridges and will fight to the last man. We will not be taken prisoner, for we have all heard the story of the crucified Canadian and the Irishman with his eyes gouged out. These stories may have been spread purposely to prevent us fraternizing. On the other hand they may be true. We must take no risks. At last news comes through, things are going badly and unless we retire and straighten out the line, we shall be cut off and eventually taken prisoners. We object to this for it is contrary to all our traditions and have we not already decided to fight to the last, but apparently we cannot afford to lose men as prisoners for they will all be needed if the Germans are to be prevented from passing Ypres.

Polygon Wood is a place of pilgrimage for many families whose ancestors fought in the war. Australian and New Zealand memorials are hidden amongst the woodland, together with headstones from many other places of the Commonwealth.

We commence to wreck the trench. Fire parties are detailed to different points with cans of petrol to fire the woods when we depart but the rain frustrates this plan. A few volunteers remain behind and from time to time put up a Verey light and a burst of fire whilst the main party silently steal away. We are in the open now with nothing between the enemy and ourselves, and those who can, move quickly for if he should discover we have gone and decides to follow it will mean hand to hand fighting with numbers in the enemy's favour. Some cannot keep the pace and limp painfully behind, but not a word is spoken. There is nothing to guide us and the night is inky dark and made worse by the drizzling rain. We enter a copse and the going is worse, the trees and tangled undergrowth impede our progress. A cry of pain rings out and I hasten my pace. A voice is pleading for succour. I grasp the arm of a comrade, we cannot ignore this call. We are alone now just two comrades and we search for him who pleads. We find him stretched on the ground and grasping his private parts as if in fear that he has lost them. We cut away his trousers and feel the warm blood oozing from a jagged hole in his thigh which we plug with a field dressing and bandage but we can still feel the blood oozing away so we put a lanyard round his thigh and twist it tight with a stick from a tree. He is forgetful in his pain and lights a cigarette which we roughly knock from his grasp and curse him for the fool he is. He cries and begs us not to leave him. We carry him as best we can, the whole three of us crashing to the ground when coming unexpectedly

upon a crater full of water. We struggle on it seems for an eternity before we come upon some stretcher bearers who relieve us of our burden. We pass through men digging - strange men they appear in the darkness. Some have beards and some appear to have turbans under their hats. In fact, I begin to wonder if I am becoming unbalanced, but it is true what I have seen for my comrade corroborates it. We rest awhile in a ditch exhausted, but not for long. Slings of cartridges are passed along and each man carries as many as he can, a tin of bully beef each and some dog biscuits, a piece of cheese, what a luxury. It is muddy and hairy, but a luxury nevertheless; a sand bag full of tea and sugar mixed. We grab a handful and put it loose in our pockets or haversacks. We haven't seen any bread lately. We are told it is issued. It probably disappears before it reaches us. We cannot grumble for we are scroungers all. A roll call of the Platoon is hastily called and many names are missing. By now this is taken for granted and does not cause consternation as at the beginning. The officer in command of our Platoon is in a shocking condition and although willing is unfit to continue. He is therefore detailed to take the casualties and the sick to the rear. We wish them God speed and envy them nevertheless, but fate is cruel and relentless, for a shell fell among them when crossing the Square at Ypres and few survived. There are no spare officers to fill the gaps so this leaves me in command of the Platoon. There is precious little commanding to be done, however, it is a case of mucking in and the devil take the hindmost. Forward again into hastily dug trenches where we had seen those strange men digging. There is a single belt of barbed wire in front and the trenches are only about two feet deep and here we are left to repel the oncoming wave when dawn breaks.

How we worked to strengthen the position. How we dig as we have never done before for we were all too few and the line very thinly held. What will the dawn reveal? Are they waiting under cover of darkness, waiting in massed formation and will they just swarm over us like locusts, faster than we can shoot them down. Dawn, mystic word. A year ago a wonderful word, a word full of romance, of adventure, now a terrible word, full of tragedy and pessimistic thoughts. Never before had I realized that dawn could break in so many ways, so many terribly beautiful ways, but just before the dawn when the mind ponders in a sloth of despond, when things which at other times seem things of beauty seem ugly and black, when trivial things seem of gigantic and overwhelming importance, when one's own breathing startles one, and the movement of a rat makes the hair stand upright. Is all this struggling worthwhile? Would it not be easier to stand on the parapet and bare the chest to the breeze until an enemy bullet would finish the struggle, but even this requires courage and I am not sure that I possess this noble quality. Do other fellows have this feeling just before dawn I wonder, or is it a sign of cowardice in me? If so, I have managed to conceal it so far and yet I am faced with the same danger as my comrades, and have they not been shot down by my side, and have I not been soaked with their precious life blood? A little stronger pull on the trigger and it would have been me. It is confusing. I cannot come to any logical conclusion.

We are ready. No sign comes through the grey mist and as we watch with rifle ready, the mist clears and we are heartened for it is plain that we have a strong position on rising ground with a good field of fire. We look across a valley. The rising ground at the other side is covered with mustard flower giving the landscape a yellow coat. Woods fringe the fields, but there is plenty of open ground so that we cannot be taken unawares. One thing is missing - the enemy, the enemy whose blood we are waiting to spill. What is he waiting for? A solitary figure emerges from a wood across the valley and fingers curl round triggers, but not a shot is fired. He strolls leisurely through the mustard fields with rifle slung over his shoulder. He wears our uniform and equipment. What does it mean? Is it a trick? He approaches our wire and is recognised as one who is reported missing. We cut the wire and let him through. He is excited and not a little scared and then we hear his story. He had been shirking his duty and fallen asleep in a dugout. Upon awaking he returned to the trench and found it empty and wondered what had happened and so not knowing what to do he had made his way back. We compliment him for his sang-froid and tell him he is lucky to get away with it but it is again only a respite, a prolongation of the struggle, for his name is exhibited in letters of gold on a roll of honour in a pawnbroker's shop, at first in a prominent position, but as the years roll on it is gradually receding into a dark corner with the cobwebs and dust.

The enemy is wary and still does not show himself. He probably does not know we have gone, or suspects a trap, or maybe waits for darkness again. Anyway the respite gives us a chance to improve our position, to make a communication trench down into the woods in rear and when the sun breaks through with its welcome and cheery warmth, we are able to make trips into the wood where water can be found, to shave off our beards, to wash our dirty faces and bloodshot eyes, to remove the filthy mud from our hands, to drink hot tea in huge quantities, to put on dry socks which we have kept carefully guarded in our haversacks. Some remove their shirts and vests and start delousing for we are all as lousy as cuckoos, even the lice are at war with us and give no quarter. We scratch ourselves with our hand until we are raw, we rub against the side of the trench but still no relief, the armpits, the navel, the private parts, where warmth is greatest are seething nests of constant irritation, the extra warmth of the sun seeming to increase the movement of these persistent parasites. Why, they even seem to flourish and increase with applications of insect powder and ointment. The birds twitter in the trees strangely out of keeping with the war-scarred surroundings and all the time the shells roar and moan overhead. They have not ceased it seems for weeks. They must be making an awful mess where they land. There must be some method in all this preparation. Is it that they are cutting us off from all communications and when their preparations are complete, they will crush us out of this ghastly salient. Another dawn and enemy patrols begin to show themselves. We hold our fire until they commence digging in about 500 yards across the valley and then commence rapid fire. Those that escape take cover in the woods. Another patrol gets fairly close under cover of a hedge partly decked in green. These suffer the same fate as the others, but still they come. They are crawling through the mustard and return our fire with disturbing effect, so we become more wary and hold our fire until a party in fairly close formation comes into view in the open. They are more careful now and appear to be moving stores through the woods. They are certainly not afraid to show themselves and work with method and system. Large armoured shields are being pushed by invisible hands to the spot where we had caught them earlier and under cover of these a trench system is started and our rifles are mere toys against this device. Troops can be plainly seen coming across the skyline in large numbers, but it is useless to waste our ammunition until they get at close range. It is quite plain that they mean business which our withdrawal had upset. Their shrapnel is now beginning to find us, the trench being narrow this does not cause many casualties. Snipers and good marksmen at that are beginning to trouble us more. There is a peculiar object in front like a man leaning on a hut and although I have registered several hits it still remains and when bullets begin to throw the dirt up into my eyes I conclude it is a dummy purposely to attract attention whilst snipers claim their victims. So I warn the men to leave it alone. There is a tall short-sighted officer in the Platoon on our left. He wears glasses. He too has seen the object and comes along to get a closer view. I air my views but he is credulous and insists that I shall register a hit while he spots but with his windowed eyes one might as well register for a blind man and when the dirt again strikes my face I tell him so quite plainly and what is more hand him a spare rifle. He calls upon a private. I object, he insists, I curse, he commands and before the shot is fired a comrade's blood and brains splash the soil and he lies inanimate at the bottom of the trench. I point the finger, an accusing finger, a finger which pours out all my hate and scorn and bitterness. He looks vacantly at me through those windows. I could bash them with the butt of my rifle, and a few hundred yards away is our common foe. He departs. We cover our fallen comrade with a waterproof sheet and there he must lie until dark for there is not room to carry him along the trench. When it is dark we will lift him gently over the back of the trench and bury him on the edge of the wood. When we must of necessity pass over him we will tread on him as gently as we can for there is no alternative.

A little to the left in a square solid brick building which appears to have escaped the shells and under cover of this the enemy are massing. This is going to give trouble, if not today it will be a nasty spot after dark. We hear that the artillery have an observer with the next platoon and a cheer goes up when with a few bumps the roof structure disappears, but the enemy still keep cover until a high explosive shell drops just at the back. At this a few break cover and in their haste present good targets for our fire. The next shell bursts right inside the roofless walls and the whole structure collapses and a tomb remains. Somewhere in Germany telegrams will be received with the dread news that someone dear is reported missing. This is not so bad as death for there is still hope, and so they will hope on, when hope is dead. A comrade good and true and an old workmate reports trouble with a sniper and as a warning to others scribbles a rough notice which he prepares to fix in a prominent spot, the sniper is too quick, and the warning lies at the bottom of the trench with the comrade's dead body. He has paid for his altruism with his life, another soul departed and another bloody body for the burial party at the edge of the wood at its back of the trench tonight. There will be no burial service with lanterns as with warriors of old, just a simple reverent prayer and if possible a rough cross marked R.I.P with indelible pencil.

Another day breaks and the enemy dawn fire is now concentrated on the trenches. The shells that have passed overhead for weeks are now dropping into and at the back of the line, but for some fortunate reason we are just on the fringe where apart from whiz-bangs, which are delivered in batches at intervals, little harm is done and then the dread word comes along passed from mouth to mouth GAS! We hastily fix our improvised pads and wait for the worst. A terrible din is going along by Polygon Wood. The gas can be seen rolling along the ground like a slow moving wave eagerly filling every hole as does the incoming tide and reluctantly breaking and rising a little when striking the trees that seem to resist its progress. Again we are fortunate for we are just on the fringe and as it endeavours to roll along the trench we beat it out with waterproof sheets and hats and any odd thing that is handy. Surely nothing can live in the centre of that cloud that slowly but surely rolls on as though proclaiming to those that wait, there is no hurry. Go whilst you have the chance. If they do go our flank will be exposed so we work feverishly to make the communicating trench into a fire trench where we can enfilade the enemy when they come through. There is no question of retiring for we have been taught that we do not retire without orders and anyway there does not appear to be anybody with authority to give such an order, and if they did, few would obey for we are fairly safe here whereas if we attempt to retire the enemy barrage is behind us so in a state of isolation we wait but the German hordes seem loath to advance. They are probably waiting, waiting to make sure that their dastardly poison gas has completed its deadly work before they come over. Perhaps they fear to look upon men dying in terrible agony as a result of their dastardly act, an act which isolates all laws of war and humanity. At last they come and we are probably more surprised than the advancing Germans when machine guns and rifles suddenly burst forth mowing them down and breaking up their advance repeatedly until the attempt is given up.

Towards evening we send a patrol to establish connection with the troops on our left. They are in a pitiable condition. The gas has claimed an appalling toll and there are sights too ghastly to depict, or ever forget, but those that are left, still doggedly defend the shattered earthworks. When darkness falls it is apparent that things have not gone so well towards the sea for the Verey lights are further back than they were last night. This is the seventh consecutive Sunday we have spent in this cruel salient and it seems an eternity. On our right is a Regiment of Regulars, well-seasoned troops who have seen service in many parts of the globe and strange are the stories they tell, and as you listen they will steal your bootlaces if you are not on guard. They have a secret society and a small party meets each night in a quiet spot at the back of our trench. Their implements consist of a rifle, a loaded sandbag, and a field dressing. They draw lots and there is usually a casualty with a bullet through the hand or the foot, either is good enough for Blighty. The fact that there is no scorching or cordite proves that the rifle was not fired at close range - the sandbag could a tale unfold.

Relief! Relief which we began to think would never come, and now it has arrived we are not excited and overjoyed as we thought we would be. We have become integral parts in this scheme and it seems all wrong that others will fill in the cogs of the gears that drive this machine. Every step is an effort, a struggle against fatigue, the march of automatons, weary bodies laden with full packs and rifles, bodies that automatically sway from side to side allowing first one leg to swing forward and then when the foot touches the ground, to prevent the body falling, the body sways to the other side the other leg repeats the process. As fatigue gains its mastery, the legs do not give way and crumple up, instead the whole body falls rigidly and in its flight strikes against another body which causes it to rebound and all the time the legs swing left, right, left, right, and the mass maintains its drunken equilibrium. This fatigue is not comparable to sore feet, it is different, one could walk on tin-tacks, there is no pain, just dull, deadly fatigue. Frequent halts are called, and when the word is given to move again, it requires a good deal of effort to regain the automatic motion which causes us to progress. We are buoyed up with the rumour that buses are waiting to carry us back for a rest, so on we tramp, on through what once was Ypres, now heaps of ruins, and shell craters full of burning debris into which are cast the dead carcasses of horses. How different to when we left it at Easter. We leave it behind us again but not with the same regret that we left it before. Hopes rise high when the familiar sight of a fleet of omnibuses comes into sight and we halt alongside. The sight seems to take us back to civilization at one bound, now at least weariness is at an end for a time. We rest awhile and then again the word comes to move, so we are not to ride in buses after all. No, these are to bring up fresh "cannon fodder" who are being thrust into the breech. We are merely the flotsam and jetsam that has escaped the tempest lay cast upon the strand clear of the waves, waves that will break again and drag us back.

We are entering a meadow and commands are being given which we automatically carry out, and then like cattle, we sink down on the grass and oblivion follows. We do not even pile our rifles, some still have them slung across the shoulder as they lay. Awaking from this sleep cold, stiff and numbed we cast off our equipment and chafe back into circulation by stamping of feet and rubbing of hands, the cooks come into their own again, fires are burning, dixies of delicious coffee are brewing, bacon is frizzling and the aroma floats into the morning air with such a delightful fragrance that I have never experienced before; wonderful white bread, tinned butter, condensed milk, jam, food, and plenty of it, and free from the filthy soil which permeates all food and drink in the trenches. There is only one fly in the ointment, this beastly chlorinated concoction which is put into the water, the taste always revives memories of the flavour of water taken from shell holes in which portions of dead men may lurk.

The sun has power now and we strip and expose our bodies to its caresses, oblivious to all other things, forgetting the inferno from which we have just escaped, oblivious of our brothers still in it, oblivious to the thunder of the guns, just to live in the sun's rays. I have never before realized how wonderful it is. The bodies look pale in spite of the dirt, but after a good mud bath and a dip in the glistening water at the bottom of the meadow, the colour returns. Our joy is short lived for now we are out of the line discipline is tightened. We must shave, clean our equipment, rifles, clothes, boots. We must fall in and number. We must slope arms, and order arms. Why the hell can't they leave a man alone until he gets his breath. No! Some big pot has to justify his job, his luxurious motor car, his chauffeur, his servant, his orderlies. He will inspect us and tell us what fine fellows we are. We grouse, but we shall obey orders and march into hell if ordered to do so.

There is no rest out of the line. Even on a Sunday the Padre must justify his existence. More cleaning and forming fours and drilling and dressing and then the greatest farce of all - we listen to the word of God disseminated by the Padre in a form to suit the occasion, the word of God, God the man of peace, of love, of goodwill towards all men, and we who have the blood of our fellow men upon our shoulders, soldiers we are called, by any name but murderers. Most of us reverently believe in the Supreme Being, and many the silent appear for succour when the thread by which we hang has become most frayed, but why? Why thrust upon us this hypocrisy? Why invoke the aid of the Deity the while we stand with weapon in hand waiting to destroy another of his creation? It would be better to leave us alone and not awaken such thoughts. There can be no uplift in war such as this, such thoughts tend to weaken the resistance.

The investigation does not take place for the wind has favoured another gas attack and in spite of the arrival of fresh troops, the position is extremely critical and as we find ourselves humping a pack back again to the salient, a dispatch rider pulls up his motor cycle at the head of the column. The column halts, and after awhile we retrace our steps, we shall not be needed after all.

O Glorious sun, all our thanks, O garb of nature in thy many colours, thy fields of green pastures, thy hedges, trees, blossoms upon which our eyes have now turned to feast. We march along with a steady rhythm, we sing, we talk. Locre, Steenwerck, Armentières. We cross and recross the Franco-Belgium frontier. At night we bivouac in the fields, we visit the Estaminets, we drink, we feed, we play cards, we bath, we delouse. We get clean underwear. It is not such a bad war after all, we get newspapers from home and according to their reports we are steadily winning and it will soon all be over. In the trenches, out of the trenches, we have at any rate lost one enemy for a season, winter with its mud and its frostbite, frostbite which at first does not appear very harmful but after months spent in hospital ends in amputation of the toes and sometimes the feet, amputation a little at a time just to keep in advance of the rot until it is arrested. Even the lice do not trouble us so much now we have laundries and can get clean underwear and our uniforms fumigated.

O Mademoiselle from Armentière
Never been kissed for umpteen years

Doo dee doo dee doo dah doo
O Mademoiselle from Armentière
Tore up her xxxxx for souvenirs
Doo dee doo dee doo dah doo

Armentières, life, movement, women and wine, its civilians still carrying on, business as usual, gay, the kiddies singing their favourite ditty

Après la guerre finis
Tout les Anglais parlez
Mademoiselle Francais beaucoup pleuring
Avec petit bebé

And of course their constant demand for souvenirs.

But a stone's throw away a war was raging and many a trench system separating these people from its terrors, they just shrug their shoulders and exclaim "C'est la guerre".

May - June 1915 Armentières area

The trenches are luxurious. They are not enfiladed or overlooked, the communication trenches are deep and wide, with camouflaged screens at all spots where the enemy are likely to observe movement. They are clean and the sanitation is good, the shelters area have beds and furniture, looted no doubt from deserted houses. It is possible to buy wine and stores from civilians at the entrance to the longest communication trench. Life is good and things are quiet. My health causes me uneasiness. My frame usually lean has suddenly developed an extraordinary stoutness and the bigger I get the weaker. My comrades insist I should see the doctor but this I cannot do or they will say of me as they do of all who report sick, "Cold feet"! and then they smirk and look knowingly at each other. No, I will hang on whilst I can stand, but even this is difficult and causes much pain. An officer converses with me. I know what he is going to say. He is going to suggest that I go back to Armentières to see the M.O. I know by his manner he is working round to the subject. I who had visions of honour and glory, and the most I could boast was a mention in despatches, if I went sick now. The war might be over and my opportunity lost before I returned, and the degradation. Wounds were considered something to be proud of, but to go sick and desert ones comrades, what would they think? I am sent back on orders with an N.C.O. as escort. The M.O. examines me and takes my temperature. He reads his thermometer and looks surprised. He gets a fresh one and takes it again, and again looks surprised. He orders me to lie on a stretcher, he dismisses the N.C.O. with the information that he can strike me off the ration's strength. Now commences a process of which I remember little, rumbling over the metalled roads on a stretcher in a G.O. wagon, temporary hospital motor ambulance, general hospital,

Red Cross Convoy, Hospital ship, Convoy again and I am among sweet-smelling white sheets, and in London too.[3] There are flowers on the tables, and dainty nurses in uniforms, and other girls too, visitors. They come and speak to me but I do not know them. They are friendly and nice to me. I suppose that is because I am a soldier. The days pass pleasantly and my only dread is that it is all a dream and that I shall suddenly awake and find myself peering into the darkness at those dead Germans that still hang on the wire. There is much suffering among the wounded and I feel ashamed that I am merely broken for a time by sickness. There are some fellows who are able to walk and not being confined to bed make themselves useful about the ward. They will bring a water bottle or a bed-pan when the nurses are busy. Sometimes they will converse and confide, I ask one fellow, "What is your trouble?" He had an attack of malaise in the street and was brought in by the Police. He also had another trouble - he was posted to a draft for the front line and had deserted, afterwards joining another Regiment. He was now wondering how much the authorities knew. So he hadn't been wounded. Another fellow had a toe removed. He confided that he was now applying for dental treatment which would mean another month and after that he was going to complain of piles. So he hadn't been wounded, he hadn't even been to the front and when he had exhausted all his lead-swinging repertoire, he had hopes of getting his discharge with a pension and he was not alone. How disgusting.

Motor drives to Raneleigh and Hampton Court, tea parties, putting parties, in fact a real good time.

July - December 1915, 3/1st Cambridgeshire Regiment. Early 1916, Army Ordnance Corps

Home again, things are going on very comfortably. The first mad rush of the hoarders has spent itself and the food supply is normal. The Army has a scale of dependants' allowances which with a little addition allows one to live. Mother looks older and grayer. I can see what she is suffering, a suffering which neither money nor food can assuage. I have noticed it in the eyes of many mothers and have purposely avoided them, it is embarrassing. She is pleased to see me, the tears run down her cheeks, she is still fearful. She runs her hands over me to see if anything is missing. I reassure her and tell her what a fine time I have had and that it will soon be over. I enquire of my brother, he too is a soldier, a married man with a family. He has not gone to war yet and I am glad. He is impetuous and of a fateful disposition and the last time I saw him I seemed to detect the same look I saw in the eyes of the fellow that stopped a bullet at the Brasserie. I hope he won't have to go. Active young men are still at the Works[5], and at the Depot a new army of clerks are installed. They have all the plums and mean to hang on to them. I soon tire of the monotonous task of training recruits and I am told quite plainly by these new soldiers who have all the soft jobs and mean to keep them, that if I want promotion I must go back to my own Battalion. So this is the

POST CARD

This Space for communication

The address to be written here

Dear Ma
Just a card to tell you
I shall probably be home for the
week-end, you might let Bert know
so that I shall be sure and see him
we are sending a draft this week
but I am not going, as you [illegible]
Reg.

Mrs Stanley
23 Ferry Path
Cambridge

POST CARD

Correspondence

Address

Dear Ma.
I may be delayed
so don't be surprised if
I do not turn up.
Reg.

Mrs Stanley
23 Ferry Path
Cambridge

Sergeant Stanely is using 3/1st Battalion Cambridgeshire Regiment postcards, though he has joined the Army Ordnance Corps by this time, to be able to return to action.

new esprit-de-corps, very well I will take my discharge and join another unit which with its lighter duty will enable me to regain my health. The winter spent in new training in and around London passes very happily and the snow still lies on the high ground on Salisbury Plain when in 1916 I am posted to a new unit preparing for service. They gave their service as Territorials and wish to go no further. A great General, but aged, calls upon them to go, and at once, and a great shout goes up No! Has the fair name of Englishmen fallen so low? There is great consternation and the General turns away, a tear glistens on his cheek and he brushes it away with his sleeve. They will go nevertheless. There are Scottish troops among them and wearing[6] the kilt. They are told they must conform and wear the regulation uniform but a shout goes up that "they can tak away our kilt but we'll ne wear the trousen", but they do and they go to the war. My head is close cropped in the German style and as I am the only one who has ever seen service in this war, it soon catches on. The Sergeant Major, an old sweat with much service and an ex pugilist, is the last to catch the vogue. He is too conservative to allow the Regiment barber to crop him so in a weak moment he allows me to do the needful. I clip his hair with a pair of clippers from the stores and his rugged head presents a comical sight when I have finished. He is now as bald as a badger. When he enters the mess a cheer goes up, a thing unheard of before in the Sergeant's Mess. He calls for a mirror and when a waiter brings one and he regards himself he is mad with rage and vows a terrible vengeance. I am saved by my comrades and seek shelter in a neighbouring mess until his wrath abates.

Spring 1916 Army Ordnance Corps, 61st Division

Once again the familiar sights. Southampton, Havre, Boulogne, Calais, St. Omer, but this time I ride in a carriage in comparative comfort whilst the troops still travel forty to a truck or alternatively eight horses. We detrain at a Railhead, unshaven, unwashed and hungry. The Sergeant Major grumbles and I ask how long are we staying here and he says two hours. "Well, may I go into the village and have a meal?" He looks at me like someone regarding a madman and demands what sort of a meal can be obtained in these foreign parts. I assure him that if he will get the Colonel's permission I will assure him a good meal. He obtains the Colonel's reluctant permission and off we set with a runner in attendance. We enter an Estaminet where I demand egg and chips, a wash and shave and our boots to be cleaned. We return to the Battalion spick and span soldiers, with bellies well filled and from then onwards my reputation is assured. Merville, La Gorgue, Estaires, Laventie, the children still play in the streets, scampering for shelter when shrapnel patters in the roofs, or spent bullets from enemy aircraft crack the tiles. Our armament has seen a wonderful change: aircraft swarm like flies, observation balloons known as sausages are dotted all along the line, heavy guns, light guns, trench mortars of all kinds. Stokes guns, wonderful contrivances fashioned like a piece of rainpipe and as fast as the shells can be dropped into them so they depart on their errand of death; Vickers Machine Guns which when full with cartridge belts will deal out death faster than the tick of the clock; Lewis Guns like outsize rifles and as the drum spins round death bursts forth to be followed by another burst as fast as a new drum is thrust on its pivot; Hotchkiss Guns with their long fretted clips of death which seem eager to do their deadly work; Mills Bombs, a stock of which can be carried in the haversack and with a little judgement can be made to explode at any point and any second, Mortars which by a pull of the trigger will land a bomb like a large plum pudding into the enemy trenches, Bangalore Torpedoes which can be pushed though the enemy wire and when exploded create a gap through which the waiting bombers rush if they are not mown down by machine guns first. Gas is used freely by both sides now and a system of alarms established. Gas masks have been improved and everyone carries the precious article, even the little children that play in the streets have regular instruction in their use. In front of Laventie and around by Richebourg things are quiet. The Portuguese have a division in this sector, known intimately as pork and beans but not disrespectfully for this gallant little nation at least has guts, guts enough to lend a hand however small and God knows a division in these times makes all the difference, whereas our proud English speaking cousins, the Americans, still proudly hold aloof. I suppose they are waiting until they bleed us to death in exchange for their trashy munitions, munitions avoided by the Troops when they learn the bitter lesson - a machine gun will stop at a perilous moment because the cartridge won't fire. This ammunition is soon recognized by its marks and dumped. A shell will explode prematurely before it leaves the gun and if it doesn't kill the gun team it will put the next gun of the Battery out of action. Ah! Well, Jerry knows a bit about soldiering, anyway he's up against a big packet this trip and he knows how to deal with it.

Our troops now have steel helmets, which are appreciated, but when some brainy individual introduced chain mail curtains to hang from the helmets to protect the eyes the limit was reached. If many more devices are added the troops will require self-propelling chairs to enable them to move from point to point, and so thousands of pounds are flogged, or buried beneath the luckless soil of France. If the Railhead will not receive stores and a Division cannot carry these, there are two channels of escape: one is to flog them to civilians, the other to dig a big hole and bury them.

French friends, including Mary le Grande and Mary le Petite, a comrade and children of the french friends.

Mary is a strapping lass and full of winning ways. Her sister is petite and droll hence the nicknames Mary le Grand and Mary la petite. A quaint and profound soul is Henri the brother. He is deaf and dumb but by following carefully his lip movement much of interest can be gained. These poor people have suffered. They have been prisoners in the German hands until a sudden thrust by the British enabled them to escape back to their home where they remain content within a mile of the line. They speak no ill of the Germans except the hatred inherent in them and fostered by their school teaching. I gather roses for Mary as I return from the line and I am allowed to sleep in a room in the house. The room is tended with care by her busy hands and I am envied by my comrades who comment knowingly to each other that I am well in, they are wrong anyway. Each night the family bids me Bon Soir in turn before they retire to sleep in the cellar and Mary la petite demands, "S'il vous entendiez les Allemandes bombard veuillez-vous frappé à la porte?" and I respond, " Oui, Mary. Bon soir."

I am not a very good watch dog for I slumber profoundly and the sun is well up when I awake to see the small white face of Mary la petite pressed against the window pane the while she hammers on the glass with her small hands. "No bon. S - levez vous, les Allemands bombard." A German battery is concentrating on an 18 pounder battery about 200 yards on our left. There is not much to fear for the German Gunners are dead on the mark and completely destroy two guns. By a stroke of luck the other two have been up wire cutting and have not yet returned. Fresh divisions are moving into position and more Artillery are getting their guns into position and there is general talk of a big advance, there is talk of an enormous concentration away on the Somme and mysterious things called Tanks of which much is expected. Everybody is optimistic of an early advance and I discuss the possibility with Mary le Grand, but she is doubtful, the characteristic shrug of the shoulders and off she goes full steam ahead. "Always zee same thing, domorrow zee big advance, domorrow zee gueurre finis, mais mon Dieu, donight encore bombard, encore zee pauvre soldat come back wiz wounds, quell malheur, O la la, zee guerre nevaire finise." Well we shall see.

The guns open out. They are putting over a barrage, our troops go over tonight, for the first time in a big do and the tension is reaching breaking point. They will be all right once they get over. It is the terrible tension of waiting, waiting for what, I thank the fates that I shall not go with them. I am entrusted with many intimate commissions if the worst should happen, and for many it will. The news comes through that they have gained their objective, the wounded are already coming back, and then it starts all over again and our troops are literally blown out of their objective. The dressing stations and clearing stations are working at high pressure and many of the wounded who have managed to get back seek shelter with the civilians until the worst cases are cleared. Mary and her party are making hot coffee for those that can take it and with their wounds roughly dressed they sit and lay around in this store room. It is a bloody scene on such a summer's night and as one walks about, the blood pads on the soles of the boots until the usual spotless tiles resemble a slaughter house. The windows are well shuttered and the oil lamps glow warmly. The heat is oppressive. Mamma, and Petit Mary and poor deaf and dumb Henri are all helping this collection of suffering humanity. The wounded nearly all smoke cigarettes, automatically, with a dazed, far away look in their eyes. They do not feel all the pain yet, they are still animals. When their mentality returns to somewhere near normal and the dressings, and the pluggings, and the probings, and the tubes come along with monotonous regularity, then war appears in yet another garb. Quel Malheur Monsieur. Toujours la même chose, toujours la guerre finis, toujours plus encore soldats blessé, pauvres garcons, Mon Dieu, Mon Dieu, la guerre jamais finis. "Who's there? Lend a hand", a stretcher bearer calls. We help then in with their burden. They are on their way to the dressing station. Their burden is a young officer. He has stopped breathing. They try to revive him but it is too late. I remember him, gay and debonair. I search his pockets. Mary would restrain me, not so my own countrymen. I am no robber of dead men. I have a reason, I am rewarded. I extract a collection of post cards, some works of art, others a little beyond. Anyway, ashes tell no tales. He was one of the best.

A breathing space behind the lines and damaged masonry provides a suitable frame for photographs. Sergeant Stanley, now with the Army Ordnance Corps, takes his turn in front of the camera for this photograph.

Weeks and months pass by and a terrible battle is raging on the Somme. So far we have escaped that sector. Between Richebourg and Bethune there lives a peasant farmer. He is getting old now but he still farms his lands. In the evenings he loves to tell us yarns of the war of 1870 when the German invaders swept across his lands and held the country to ransom. Ah!, says he as he ruminates. It is different this time. We have gallant Allies who hold him and will beat him for the last time. Poor old fellow. [Post script: He was right in one thing - the Allies beat him all right but I often wonder what became of the poor old fellow in 1918 when once again in his lifetime the Boche swept across his lands and destroyed a lifetime's endeavour, and yet these people still cling on with the sword suspended over their heads.]

We are resting in Merville and I decided to look up Mary at the old billet. A change has taken place and the laughter has disappeared. It is afternoon and Mary is drinking beer. She refuses to be cheered and parrot-like reiterates "C'est la guerre". I search for Henri and he seems gloomy. By signs and lip movements I demand what is wrong with them all. What has become of the joking, the leg-pulling and the laughter. He commences his business of signs and lip twisting. "No bon, no bon. Officiers' mess ici maintenant, quand Mary met le diner sur la table, tous les officiers comme ca", and by a movement of his hand he made it quite clear what the officers did. "Vraiment Henri?" "Oui Monsieur en verité, vous savez Monsieur les officiers Allemands no bon mais jamais comme ça. C'est la guerre, c'est la guerre". I try to explain to Henri that in all communities one will find good, bad and indifferent, but this does not console him.

Summer - Autumn - Winter 1916

The summer passes and the bloody struggle continues and as Mary would say the "war never finishes" and with winter approaching we find ourselves on the Somme. Martinsart where the heavy guns shake the cellars in which men sleep, where enormous rats fight for food under the wire beds and if vigilance is relaxed they will gnaw the ears as one sleeps. Along through Pioneer Road where black boys work in the sawmills. To the right lies Avuluy on the road to Albert, and to the left Beaumont and Beaumont Hamel, in front Thiepval where Howitzers bump incessantly and then over the rising ground in front, confusion. It is useless to refer to the map for the whole scene has been so well churned that nothing but mud and ghastly corruption remain. Steel helmets lay scattered haphazard, some singly and some in groups telling their own story. Here and there a derelict Tank, legs stick up with the feet still embedded in the mud, a ragged puttee blowing in the wind, a shattered leg protrudes from a German field boot, sickly hands still grasp the shattered sandbags. Here a German bomb store dug into the side of a sunken road, my colleague a Canadian is the first to explore. He is chewing tobacco, he always is. He has one foot and half his body through the opening and in this position searches pockets for some matches and when one is struck his foot is pressing on the stomach of a dead German and their faces almost touch. More with fright than

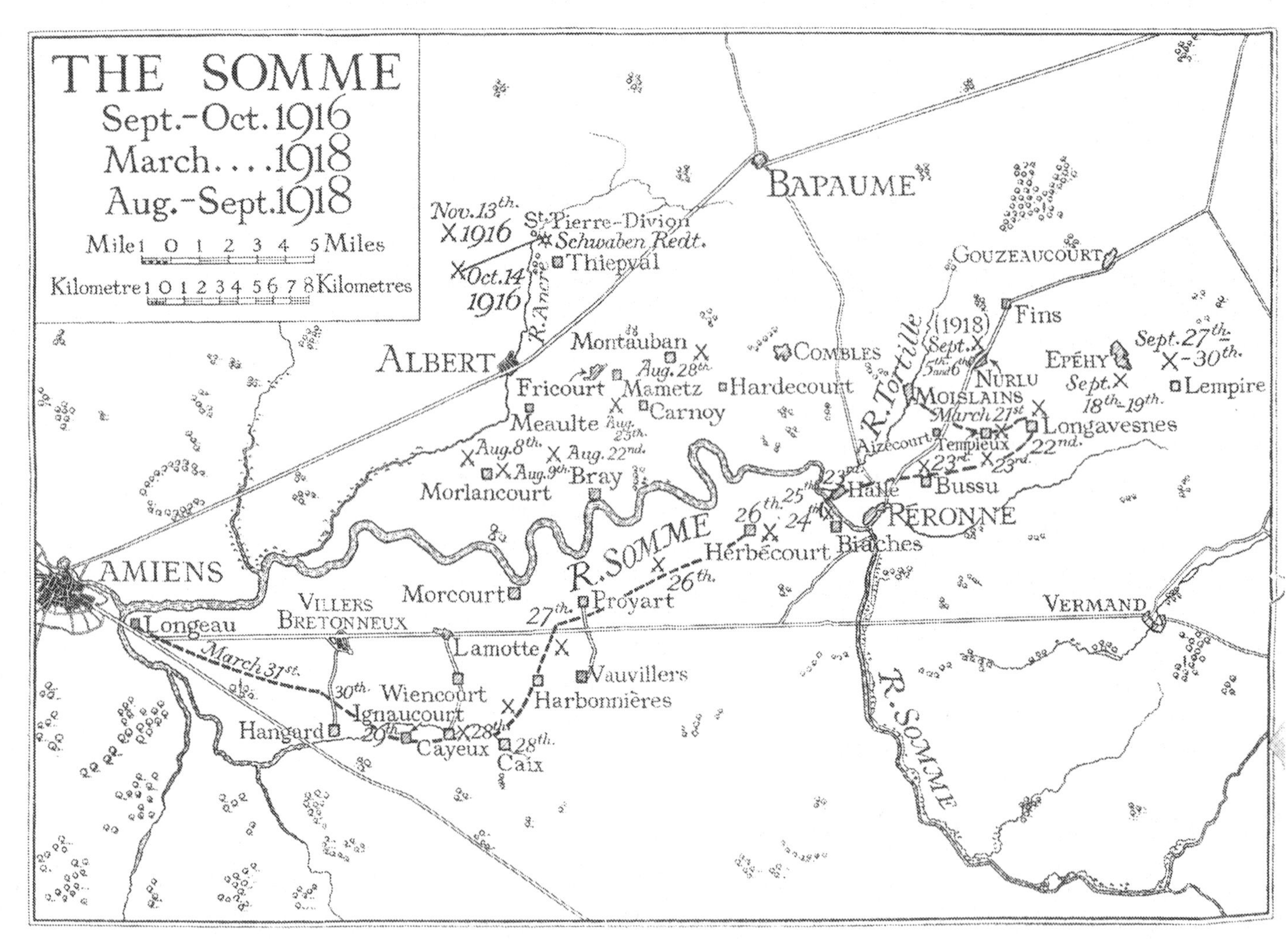

The map of the Somme area prepared by Brigadier-General Riddell and Colonel Clayton to illustrate their later account of the history of the Cambridgeshires from 1914 to 1919. Sergeant Stanley was there in the autumn with the Army Ordnance Corps.

with intent he spits out the chewed tobacco in the dead face and lifts his foot and the dead body falls back. Using more care we step over it and proceed a few paces before striking another match and there towering in the corner is another dead German, erect and leaning back against the wall still guarding his bombs. Death must have come unexpectedly, it may have been gas. Further back there are others in various positions and all laid out ready are bombs, small black bombs like eggs, stick bombs like a green jam tin on the end of a wooden stick, bombs as numerous and varied as the goods in a fancy store. The fighting has settled down again for another winter of trench warfare. A few miles have been gained at a terrible cost of manhood and we are faced with the prospect of maintaining communication over this rain soaked, mud churned, stinking desolate morass, a struggle against mud and lice where death has trod and retrod every yard, and in every form, and still stalks triumphant.

An old wound is causing me trouble and the septic is getting into my system racking me with pain and making a nightmare of the nights. The Doctor uses his lancet which gives temporary relief but afterwards gets worse. With my right hand wrapped in an old scarf I am beginning to lose in this struggle of the survival of the fittest. I cannot keep myself clean and unless something is done even the lice will gain the mastery, and again I cannot fight for my fair share of rations. We are moving back for Christmas. This is good news for I shall be able to get proper attention. The French canvas huts where we are to sleep have floors of soft mud and even this is lousy, but soft mud is not too bad to sleep upon and we at least have a roof. Across the Road is a barbed wire enclosure, with armed guards. Inside are rows of tidy well-built wooden huts, they are double walled and stuffed with sawdust. They have proper heating stoves, and kitchens, and a mess room. Even the latrines are covered in. On the whole luxurious, but not for us the victors, No! It is a German prisoner's camp where they thrive and grow fat on their plentiful rations. The prisoners look smart and clean. They have their own barber and tailor, and their lot is envied by many of our own war weary, mud begrimed troops. An orderly brings the news that I have been allotted Christmas leave to England. I am to see the M.O., get my pass from the Orderly Room and get on a train at the Railhead the same night. What luck. Christmas Day at home. The Doctor cannot let me go and informs me that I must go to Hospital. By exercising all my persuasive art and promising to report to the nearest Hospital when I get home I manage to get through, promise or no promise. I am going to spend Christmas Day at home but on Christmas morning I can stand the pain no longer and make my way to the nearest Hospital. A Sister admits me and removes the dressing and part of a finger, leaving the black bone projecting. She is annoyed and demands why I have allowed this state of things. I explain that I have just come from the Somme. She leaves me to return with the news that I must go to the Theatre. I enter and clamber on to the table. An Orderly orders me off. At this moment a Doctor and a Sister enter and order me on the table again. The Orderly explains that I have not been sterilised or something like that. Anyway, they compromise and agree that they will remove my boots and tunic. By this time I have fully entered into the spirit of the game and clamber down again. I suspect that the Christmas festivities have commenced. The Sister leans across my body and the warmth and close proximity are very comforting. Meanwhile the Doctor is busy preparing his instruments, a pad held over my nostrils and sleep ensues but not for long for I can hear voices and feel an acute soreness to my right. I turn my head in that direction and vaguely observe the Doctor removing a piece of bone. I groan and the pad is soon placed over my nostrils again. They have finished now and I get down from the table. The Orderly wraps a blanket around me and pushes me into a wheeled chair, but I will have none of it. He gains the advantage and wheels me off triumphantly and dumps me on a bed. The ward is gaily decorated and the Christmas spirit prevails. I have visions of roast turkey and flaming plum pudding and I am not disappointed. A trooper in the next bed has his leg amputated below the knee and soaks the raw stumps in a pail of some liquid, another is having the plugging and pus removed from a hole in his side, probes are busy, and tubes and pus predominate, but these things do not spoil the appetite when one is really hungry.

1917

The first months of 1917 are very severe with frost of long duration and the cause of much hardship and suffering among the Armies in the field. It is so cold that the water can be carried in sandbags in the form of ice. Hostilities on a grand scale are practically at a standstill. Patrols report that Bapaume has been evacuated but strange to say when a raiding party go over the next night strong opposition is met with. The winter begins to break although snow is still falling and signs of renewed activity can be felt in the air. The enemy is extraordinarily quiet and apart from long range shells there is no sign of life. Aircraft report that the enemy appear to be moving back and sure enough he has cleared so cleverly that the whole of this hard fought sector is now in our hands, without a shot, but what a gift, ruin and dislocation everywhere. It is more apparent than ever how grievous have been the Somme battles on both sides. Cavalry patrols push forward

In the wake of the Hun, St. Quentin (p. 62). It is one of the few photos where Sergeant Stanley tries to give us a view of the landscape. For the purposes of this publication, the sky in the picture, very marked on the original, has been cleaned up.

and Infantry advance warily. Bapaume is now in our hands and scores of rubbish heaps that once were busy villages and the enemy still appear to be going back. It really seems that they are weakening and this spring will see us victorious. Fritz is keeping up his reputation for ruthlessness. Every tree has been levelled to the ground, every well has been bombed and polluted, every cross road has been mined leaving huge craters round which detours have to be made by the transport, causing delay in communication. In spite of his running away tactics it would appear that he had made a fine art of comfort and protection - deep well constructed dug-outs proof against the heaviest shells with alternative exits, heated by specially constructed stoves with air inlets and outlets for the products of combustion, wire beds arranged in double tiers and in some cases electrically lighted which compared with the poor protection we knew and the grievous casualties caused by braziers without ventilation makes one think that the German war machine even in small details is no slipshod scheme.

The advance continues over open country and after years of trench warfare, when any yard was gained at terrible cost, every mile now seems ten and still the enemy retire We meet with a new experience as we enter the hamlets and the civilian population greets us, a trifle timidly at first for they have been in the hands of the Germans since 1914 and scarcely know what to expect next but when they find that we are willing to share our rations of food and tobacco they open their hearts and loosen their tongues and strange are the stories they tell. On the whole they do not appear to have been treated too badly but it is apparent that food and clothing have been scarce. They show signs of scurvy. Some of the local beauties have gone back with their German lovers but some still remain. There is just a suspicion that some of the tales are venomous gossip, anyway there are plenty of square headed babies. The civilian question opens up a new problem for with extending lines of communication and no railways it is no easy matter to feed civilians in addition to an Army on the move. Huge cemeteries tell the tale of the German dead and we now begin to see a little of what has been happening behind the enemy front. There is a redeeming feature in favour of the enemy in that we find our own dead buried decently and recorded with their own. This redeeming feature is soon counterbalanced by another sign of Hunnish frightfulness which nevertheless we are fools not to forsee. Some of the billets are left intact with fires ready laid in the stoves and when a match is applied a bomb in the flue does its deadly work and so all stoves are given a wide berth, but in spite of this, old enemy billets and buildings blow up at intervals until a thorough search is made and the mystery solved. Quantities of high explosive had been placed in any concealed spots and left ready detonated, a weight suspended above the striker by a wire and the wire well-wrapped with acid and rag, and there we have a glorious uncertainty. When the acid has eaten the wire away sufficiently to allow its weight to drop more names will appear on the missing list. Strangely enough the troops still avail themselves of the shelter and comfort of these billets, but for my own part I prefer a waterproof sheet or a sheet of iron in the open.

The advance slackens and finally comes to a standstill. Once again we are doomed to disappointment and find ourselves confronted with a formidable trench system. We have not broken through and the enemy is not weakening. He has merely made a tactical retirement very cleverly carried out.

Another terrific onslaught takes place in front of Arras with some local success but still the front remains unbroken and still the struggle proceeds with death and suffering torment riding rampant through the land. It seems that this thing will never come to an end. There are persistent rumours that America is still thinking about it and some have it that she is actually coming in on our side but this has been a stock joke for so long that it is treated with a pinch of snuff. Another joke is the story of the newspaper man who had seen the Privates frying steaks in the trenches, which reminds me of the Private who lived on bully beef and biscuits for a long spell, before meat and vegetables in tins were introduced. An officer coming upon the scene was indignant that the Private should swear and groan so profoundly and to prove that bully beef and biscuits were most appetizing the officer commenced to eat some, and because the Private commented that it might be very well after cold chicken and wine, he was penalized. "C'est la guerre."

There is also a good deal of talk in the papers about venereal disease and to judge by some articles one would think that the war was being fought in some prostitutes' parlour. Well after three years in the front areas, I have seen very little opportunity of contracting this grievous disease. The womenfolk in the front areas would appear as virtuous as most other communities and in the towns the brothels commonly know as Red Lamps, appear to be well regulated. One can drink and fraternise with the almost

Photos that fit with the fading of summer. The picture on the right has been framed to show the way that Sergeant Stanley wrote on the edge of the negatives; the centre picture indicates that it was taken at Amiens

nude damsels in these establishments and having, if so desired, made the choice, come to terms and paid the tax, the contract is duly carried out. Young lads to whom in some cases this is the first step from virtue return with sparkling eyes, older men also return with a look of hectic satisfaction. I have an idea that the root of the trouble is at the big base depots where men stay a long time in the same place and so have opportunity to contract illicit alliances.

The summer is fast passing and another and final effort to break the front, before another winter settles upon us, is being made in the Ypres sector, but in spite of our enormous supplies of shells and guns and the wonderful courage and heroism of the troops, gas bombs, mines, aeroplanes, tanks and any and every ghoulish contrivance to take life the same tragic story recurs: men march up singing and return wounded as fast as lorries can carry them. They return huddled together like carcasses of meat. It is quite impossible for the ambulances to deal with such numbers and they must be cleared to make room for more. The wet season is with us again now and we settle down to another winter with its mud and frostbite. There are some bright spots and the spirit and

A series of pictures of Arras taken by Sergeant Stanley, with the effect of the shelling of the town. Two of the views are taken inside the cathedral. The photo in the centre below has the words 'The great Arras sacrifice written on it - there are rows and rows of temporary wooden crosses in the background. The pictures below are of the reconstructed town today.

humour of all the ranks is wonderful but in spite of it all there is a sense of weariness and a dogged carrying on.

In moving up and down the fronts a little entertainment can be snatched from the Towns a few miles behind the lines and many of these places hold happy memories and friendships - Poperinge, Arras, Hesdin, Bethune, Nesle, Armentières, La Gorgue, Estaires, Merville, Amiens, Aily sur-Noye, Aire. We were hoping to get in one of these shows for Christmas but we are destined to spend it in desolate quarters in the Cambrai sector, but we have good food rations and plenty of food and we know by now how to make the best of it. Perhaps next year will see the end.

Friends.

The Start of 1918

1918 and so another year commences, finding us on the move again. We appear to be going farther south than we have before and finally find ourselves among the French troops before St. Quentin. The front is quiet and thinly held, the weather is bad and the billets are worse. There are no civilians around here and we look like settling down to months of rural monotony. We get to work and make ourselves as comfortable as possible. In the evening we visit our French allies. They are very convivial and always have a liberal supply of Vin Blanc and Vin Rouge. They are not good boozers and soon get excited and so tire themselves. We get a pressing invitation to visit them the following night and

"Entente cordiale" on the Somme.

not wishing to impose upon them we take a liberal supply of Rum and so the fun waxes fast and furious until we depart leaving them all as drunk as possible. The next evening we pay another visit but find them in their beds not prepared to tackle any more Rum.

The French gradually disappear and the front is now in our charge. There are still a couple of Gendarmes in a nice little hut made of sleepers at the fork roads. A friend and myself make a lot of them and treat them well for we covet their hut and they will soon depart and we hope leave us in possession. We strike a bargain and give them a tin of 50 Woodbines each and agree to look after their dog and the hut is ours. This dog is cute, it cannot speak English but it can sit up and ask for our rations all right and contrary to most dogs I have known it enjoys a drop of spirits, and the boys knowing this purposefully make it drunk. It will walk like a drunken man and roll on the ground and its progress is comical beyond belief. It will spend the night among the coal near

The dog gave several opportunities for a photograph. The picture above may well be Mary le Grande and Henri with the dog.

the stove for warmth and in the morning all black and with bloodshot eyes it will arise and take a run in the wet grass returning clean and ready for breakfast. Booze will be its undoing. It got run over once trying to cross the road while drunk. We took it to the Vet who stitched it up and so we nursed it back to health. It has become a thief now so we try to get rid of it. We put it in a passing G. S. Waggon thinking it will probably get a good billet in some transport lines but when the next day we find it outside with bleeding feet and almost exhausted we haven't the heart to again play such a scurvy trick. Anyway after stealing half a mug of rum and tea it tried to stop a lorry and the wheel went over its head.

Italian troops appear at the Railhead and we wonder what the new move is but as no more arrive we conclude that they are labour troops. There are also large gangs of Chinese labour, a most amusing crew.

The front is extraordinarily quiet but there are no signs of Infantry behind the front. Aircraft and observation balloons are everywhere and there is a feverish activity on the back areas. The general topic of conversation is that we are hard up for men and money and that there will be no big attacks this year. That's something to be thankful for anyhow, but we cannot remain here on the defensive for the rest of our lives. Honestly I'm getting a bit windy. I've been a long time out here and my colleagues are all strangers. They all get it in the neck sooner or later and when I commence to call the roll it puts the breeze up me for it must be my turn soon. The troops seem to be getting less and less. Battalions are being made up with three Company's Brigades with three Battalions and so on and reading between the lines one Army is doing the work of two and it is darkly rumoured here in the 18th Corps of the 5th Army that General Gough is being left with the baby. As a bit of camouflage we are told to dig any spare ground in our spare time, and we are actually issued with seeds and seed potatoes but I don't think there will be a very good crop for we sow stones and have chip potatoes for supper. We don't intend to let Jerry have the benefit of our labour. There is a lot of Secret Service work going on. The pigeon stations are all arranged and well tried. Rear headquarters are being thrown back. We are converting mortars into land mines as hard as we can and every night these land mines are being buried in No Man's Land and along all roads and likely spots. There is a feeling that a nasty jar is coming our way and when it does come it will be a case of every man for himself.

I get a letter from my brother, he is still in England but tells me he cannot stay there much longer. I must write to him, I cannot tell him why but he must not come out here yet he must hold on at least for another three months. He must resort to any subterfuge he can think of but he must stay in England. He is my brother and why should he be killed, but why shouldn't he fight like others have to do, but no, he must not come yet, curse the censor. Why can't I tell him why? They think we are fools and do not know but we do. Why doesn't the enemy shell us by day and bomb us by night like he does on other fronts, and why doesn't he send us some gas? No he is too good which is always a bad sign.

There is a rushing hither and thither by Gold Braided Staff Officers and all kinds of orders continue to come through of course all marked secret, quite amusing when one thinks that they are handled by every Tom, Jack and Harry. Probably regarded as wonderful Secret Service work emanating from some highly paid staff officer.

There are a couple of Parsons in a billet not far away, not bad fellows but I cannot think why we want so many for there is no work to do when the troops are in the line. They are only eating useful men's rations and occupying billets which are scarce. Perhaps I am getting bitter and losing faith in religion. When I came into this war I was inspired by the violation of Belgium and the succour of women and children but I am beginning to see through things a little. There are moneyed interests at work and it will be a sad business for so many seemingly patriotic people at home when the war finishes if ever it does. Women have come forward splendidly and are doing men's work but I have an idea in spite of their splendid heroism there will be no place for us if ever we return. We are already outcasts and almost forgotten. When we go home on leave we cannot mix with them for they are suddenly wealthy and have only the best and most expensive of things made possible by the ridiculous remuneration for so-called munition work which compared with our pay as soldiers is princely.

There is another class of women whose courage, heroism and sacrifice is deserving of the highest praise but they too appear to be forgotten: the nurses in the front areas where romance and sentiment cease to exist, where life hangs but by a thread no more, where the work which they are called upon to do is even worse than the shells and aircraft bombs which number them among their victims. There is no holding patients hands in flower bedecked rooms amid romantic surroundings where the gallant Dragoon staggers in with gold braid and a bloodstained bandage round his head. No! The work is fast and furious, filthy and bloody, abdominal cases are bad at any time but when the casualty has been snatched from a muddy, gory swamp, hardly recognizable from the mud which is everywhere, as lousy as a cuckoo, and with no control over the lower organs, the smell and the groans, it is a miracle that these women do not lose their reason.

Spring 1918

The Mechanical and Horse transport drivers and other details are having refresher courses in the use of arms and Hotchkiss Guns are being issued to them as a protection against aircraft they are told - another piece of camouflage, peashooters would be as useful for this purpose. I have spent thousands of rounds of small ammunition with tracer bullets under favourable conditions and it seems futile. Tons of anti-aircraft shells fill the air every day with as much futility. Aircraft seem to be the only weapon against aircraft and every day planes and sausage balloons crash to the ground in flames, a duel is taking place at this moment over a battery of field guns, one plane topples over and zig-zags downwards. It may be a trick to escape but no the plane bursts into flames and two figures jump clear. They have no parachutes and strike the ground with a sickening thud. They are Germans, mere boys with smooth girlish faces. I don't know why they jumped. Probably they preferred death that way rather than being burned alive. They are busy searching out our batteries but our aircraft now seem superior and have the enemy well within hand. The days lengthen and the sun has more power, apart from increased aerial activity things are practically at a standstill and as spring approaches and nothing happens we begin to think that we are mistaken and all those feverish preparations are a sign of what is known as the wind up for have we not been fed for years on the gospel that our enemies are short of everything and it is only a question of time before they give in, and besides America is supposed to be coming to help us, but like the Russians who came through Scotland in 1914 they fail to materialize. There is a new song which some of the boys brought back from leave, something about the "Yanks are Coming." I think they must be coming on foot and like the way to Tipperary it is a long, long way. (They call themselves Doughboys but although much needed they, like the Baker's dough, fail to rise.) Ah me, our information is very limited. It is early morning and I awake earlier than usual. It is misty outside probably the portent of a hot sunny day. The guns seem busy to the north and there is an unusual hubbub of rifle and machine gun fire, heavy explosions shake the ground. Perhaps some of our boys are trying some of the new land mine detonators, stones and clods of earth rattle on the roof. It is too light for aircraft bombs. I must see what is the matter so pulling on my slacks I shake my comrade who slumbers like a log and then throw open the door. To my surprise German soldiers in groups are running past the door into a sunken road to the rear. I acquaint my comrade and grasp my revolver, he still in his shirt grasping his rifle - here's a pretty predicament but the sleeper hut is sturdy and affords good cover. We will wait for the next group and do our best but when the next group appears they are without arms or equipment running like frightened hares towards our idea of where Blighty lays, probably some poor devils who came through with the first wave and finding themselves too far forward threw away their arms and took the opportunity of getting out of it. We send a message to headquarters and he returns with the information that the front is broken and every man for himself, darned absurd for there is work to be done. There is no mistaking the fact that something serious has happened for as far as the eye can see gun teams are falling back across country at the gallop, taking advantage of cover and coming into action as opportunity offers, a most unheard of thing in broad daylight. Enemy aeroplanes abound like swarms of bees swooping almost to the ground and emptying their machine guns. The Infantry are falling back fighting every inch of the way. The wounded are having a rough time for the Hospitals are clearing back, the whole thing is so sudden that many fall into enemy hands. We set to work and burn all secret documents, there are secret devices which must not fall into enemy hands. These we dump down a deep well and then a bomb follows, anyhow this is the best we can do and it will take a lot of digging to find anything. There are rifles, machine guns and ammunition, well these look like going west. Two lorries approach but they will not stop, poor fools, or lucky, they run straight into the German lines. Another approaches. He will stop or he will stop a bullet from my revolver. He stops and his lorry is full of officers' Mess furniture. We soon dump this in the road and load as many arms as we can and send him off through the sunken road. We must get away and leave the rest. Thank goodness we are under no obligation to stay. Enemy aircraft fire is bad enough but fire is coming from the rear now. We take cover and waiting our opportunity signal to our own troops, an Infantry Regiment feeling its way forward. Goodness knows what has happened to our troops that were in the line. The fresh troops dig in and we dispose of the remainder of our arms and ammunition. This is a stroke of luck and so we make our way to find our own headquarters. Aircraft and Engineers are busy blowing up our ammunition dumps and firing petrol dumps. All bridges are ready to be blown up and in the general chaos that prevails some are destroyed before all the field guns are clear. Well guns are no good without ammunition however heroic the teams and there is nothing for it but to destroy the sights and dump the loose gear. The horses can swim the river and the troops can get across on punts and rafts although many have to swim. Day after day and night after night we keep getting bumped further back and the news from the North is no more reassuring. We have indeed underestimated the enemy resources. He appears to have unlimited supplies of men and munitions. Nearly every other man appears to have a machine gun. They have lightened their heavy machine guns and advance firing from the hip with short bursts of about 30 rounds and the effect is deadly. Fresh troops appear like weeds after rain and if things continue we shall soon be pushed into the sea and find ourselves swimming for home. In spite of this state of affairs and the general chaos that prevails no fresh troops appear to be coming to the rescue. The authorities seem more concerned in destroying any supplies of intoxicants and in some places champagne runs down the gutters like water. As we enter a village the last of the civilians are leaving. It is a pitiful sight to see these people departing with as many of their goods and chattels as they can escape with. We commence a scrounging expedition and have the good luck to find a live fowl which we kill and put in a large stewpan full of water, feathers and guts included. This is not an ideal way to boil a fowl but as it is we may not have time to eat it. The feathers soon boil off and the guts give quite a good flavour to the flesh. The alarm is given and field grey cavalry can be seen crossing the horizon and we commence to get away under cover. There is a lot of truth in the old adage that he who fights and runs away lives to fight another day and when the truth is fully appreciated this factor probably played a big part in saving the situation later. At the cross roads we run full tilt into a full blown General. This is unfortunate. Whoever thought of seeing a General here anyway. He bars the way but at this moment a staff officer, probably a Brigade Major, gallops down the road towards him and the meeting is anything but cordial. The General wants to know how the staff officer expects the men to stand when he is running away and turning him about sends him back to the line with the admonition "That way your duty lies." Grave words but the General has a powerful car round the corner with its engine running. We decide to go back for our fowl and find a funny little man eyeing it greedily. He has no tunic or hat and he is drunk. His accent proclaims him to be Scotch. He insists on taking us to his dug out and in a back garden we find a miniature fort of sandbags and enough rum to sink a ship. He intends to stay and meet old Hindenberg and if he can't beat him with his fists he will square him with a jar of rum. We fail to change his mind so give him a piece of our fowl and leave him to it. We are almost drunk ourselves and have been for days, but we don't want rum when there is plenty of champagne.

I don't know what is happening to the North but we seem to be drifting sideways towards Mondidier and getting mixed up with the French troops who appear to be as hard pressed as ourselves. Towards evening we enter a Town with a railhead on the main line to Paris and to this point all the civilians are concentrating. We receive the hospitality of an old veteran of 1870 who with his wife and daughter are hanging on to the last in the hope that the retreat will stop. There is food and drink in plenty for most of the shopkeepers have fled. The old chap is sinking his sorrow with drink and the poor old lady is grief stricken. The daughter Josephine, the good Samaritan is helping all and sundry. All is hustle and the din on the metalled roads is deafening. Ammunition lorries, guns, ambulances, G.S. wagons and French Cavalry in two columns backwards and forwards, further to the edge Infantry marching forward. Old men and young boys singing and laughing - their spirits are wonderful, poor devils. There must be some amongst them who know. On the fringe all feverishly going in one direction, the refugees, the most pitiful sight of all, poor old men and women, young girls and babies, footsore, weary almost to complete exhaustion, jostling, shouting, crying, wringing their hands, some falling exhausted by the roadside, they are all in the same plight and they cannot help each other and in every eye there is the same look, the fear of the terror that urges them on. Shells are already dropping on the railhead and as fast as the Engineers repair the line at one spot it is cut at another but they work incessantly and fearlessly for if those refugees are not cleared the place will be a shambles.

Here is a poor woman in a terrible plight. She has been wheeling a baby in a perambulator all day and now one wheel has collapsed and she has fainted. We carry her into Josephine's house with the baby and while she is being nourished we manage to repair the wheel by taking a spoke from each of the good wheels. She dare not linger and off she goes again full of gratitude.

A cry goes up and everybody is chatting and gesticulating. A poor old lady has fallen from a wagon and broken her leg. We pull her aside for the traffic does not stop, we smash in a door and carry her onto a bed and apply a splint roughly for there are no doctors here. She revives after a bit but we cannot leave her here. After a good deal of trouble we manage to smuggle her into a wagon. We don't know where it is going but we don't care as long as we get the poor old girl out of this. We snatch a young Infantry officer from the rabble. He has a nasty head wound and is dazed just being carried along by the tide. We take him to our hostess to rest awhile. Josephine meantime proclaims what she would do with the Allemandes if she had the opportunity. I'm afraid she won't have the opportunity and unless she departs fairly soon she may stay for good for heavy shells are falling on the Town now. A tired Military Policeman comes along with a German prisoner and begs a meal and a rest. I am not partial to these fellows but he looks dead beat. He has lost his bearings and like many more of us is free-lancing to the best of his ability. The organization for dealing with prisoners has broken down and he doesn't know what to do with him. I suggest an easy way but the Policeman to my surprise has a heart and says it can't be done in cold blood. I hand the prisoner over to some French troops in a barn adjacent and send the Policeman in to Josephine's. In a few minutes there is a terrible hubbub and a French serjeant hauls me along to the barn and demands that I remove the German prisoner at once. Poor devil, he is crouching in a corner and the drunken soldiers are threatening him with their wicked four sided bayonets. Well, I demand of the Sergeant, why not! Oh no monsieur it is not fair twenty to one, dear me. Another man with a heart. Human nature's not so bad after all. I grab the prisoner by the cuff and haul him to his feet. He is grasping something in his other hand as I grab his wrist. It is a wallet and I look inside. There is a photograph of a woman and several children, his family I suppose. Whatever was this poor little man doing here, another victim of this cruel war machine. I will make him a present to Josephine so opening the door and pushing him in I tell Josephine here is your German and depart. I expect to see him come hurtling out into the roadway but as nothing happens I return and to my surprise find him seated at the table with our own fellow and some French civilians, devouring food and drink which Josephine has given him. He must have produced his family group, enough to soften a man's heart to say nothing of a woman's.

The memorial at Arras, designed, as were many of the cemeteries, by Lutyens.

Every day finds us a little further back and still fresh enemy troops appear on the scene but the quality is not so good. Probably a sign that every man is being used in this final gigantic effort. Orders come through that a stand must be made at all costs, something about having our backs to the wall, fine stuff for newspapers and afterwards for history. My brother is dead. He probably had his back to the wall[8]. It is of no use to moan. Every other soldier wears a black button now. Could we but return to the happy days of 1914, things can never be the same again, my brother is dead. I expected this but my poor old mother she will never be the same again. I may not even see her again. Fortunately there is no time to think.

No matter how dark the hour before dawn the sun is sure to shine again if we live to see it and at last the enemy is weakening. Order ensues from chaos, fresh troops appear on our side and at last he is stopped. But what are the prospects, a repetition of trench warfare. Looking back over the last few months events appear as a drunken nightmare. Discipline is now being tightened up and drink is not so plentiful. There is talk of Bolshevik influences being at work, a lot of tommy rot for after all flesh and blood is not steel and when the organisation breaks down and men are left to make the best of such a bloody job as this by their own resourcefulness they can hardly be expected to behave as saints. The Enemy are disseminating propaganda from aircraft but with little effect for the penalty of reading the leaflets is great and as searches are made frequently it is risky to retain any information although many take the risk as souvenirs.

What wonderful news I am to go on leave to England, this wonderful homeland for which we have been fighting these long years. Green fields, quiet fresh running rivers and streams, friends that are dear, peace and rest from this drunken topsy turvey turmoil. What dreams, alas to be dashed to the ground. Enemy aircraft bomb us incessantly on the way to the coast, even in London they will not give us rest. I call in a familiar barber's shop and whilst having a hair cut and shampoo listen to the gossip of the day, but when I am asked to pay 5/- for this small service I threaten to smash up the shop and eventually pay 2/6p. So this is one of the citizens of my beloved England for which

The Canadian memorial at Vimy has retained Allied and German trenches to give just some small feel of what this area was like during the First World War.

we sacrifice so much. My mother is broken with sorrow and deep in a lethargy which cannot be lifted. I should not have come home, it would have been better otherwise. The going away will be fresh torture to this frail little creature. I call upon my friends but am forgetful and find them not. The war has swallowed up the youth leaving only sorrowing parents and my presence only opens afresh their sorrow. I should not have come. I search for my girl friends, they have gone too. Some have married soldiers, a few are happy but many are already widows. I will seek solitude on my beloved river in a canoe, with a book for company. I will visit the haunts that I love so well but even this has lost its beauty for German prisoners have been employed cutting down the trees and removing fallen ones that laid across the stream and gave such a picturesque effect. I will stretch my limbs on the grassy banks and smoke my pipe and read in solitude. A keeper approaches and politely asks me to remove myself. I protest that I am doing no harm and surely this is our beloved England for which we fight. He has been a soldier but is now a serf and merely doing his duty. I will go, I cannot understand this new spirit. Can this be the new thing referred to as Bolshevism, these lands, this wealth, what will it avail the owner if my comrades fail? And yet I am not allowed to rest on one square foot, I should not have come home. I am not one of this community. I have lost touch with their ways. I will take my bicycle and ride into the country to visit the mother of a comrade and to keep a promise. On my return I will ask a countrywoman to make some tea for which I will pay as we do in France where the peasants make us welcome, but my efforts are met with suspicion and I am unsuccessful. I visit a local preacher. He is comfortably installed in his office. He is not too old to be of service but he escapes. He has sons and by some means they escape. He tells me how well I look and how I have got on, what a fine time we must all be having and what a draught we shall feel when it is all over. Poor religious fool. Oh that he could be made to spend a winter in the ditches down by the river, that alone would be sufficient without the mad spectre of death that rides among us as the balls in the skittle alley. I must return to France where at least we understand each other. I cannot stand any more or this or I shall go mad and run amok.

The Final Advance

Back in France a wonderful change has taken place. Men and munitions seem more plentiful than ever before, the organization seems better and in spite of the events of the spring the morale is better. We are pressing forward again now and once again we return to familiar landmarks, the enemy puts up an obstinate resistance but apart from picked snipers and special machine gun squads the old resistance is lacking. Each day brings fresh victories. There is no mistaking the trend of events this time. This is no organised withdrawal, the prisoners come through in large numbers and seem gloomy and glad to be out of it all. All their seemingly impenetrable defences are gradually giving way before the Allied attacks. Guns of all calibre and ammunition in huge quantities are left behind in their anxiety to escape. In many cases their own guns and shells are turned upon themselves, guns strew the countryside, some in their emplacements and

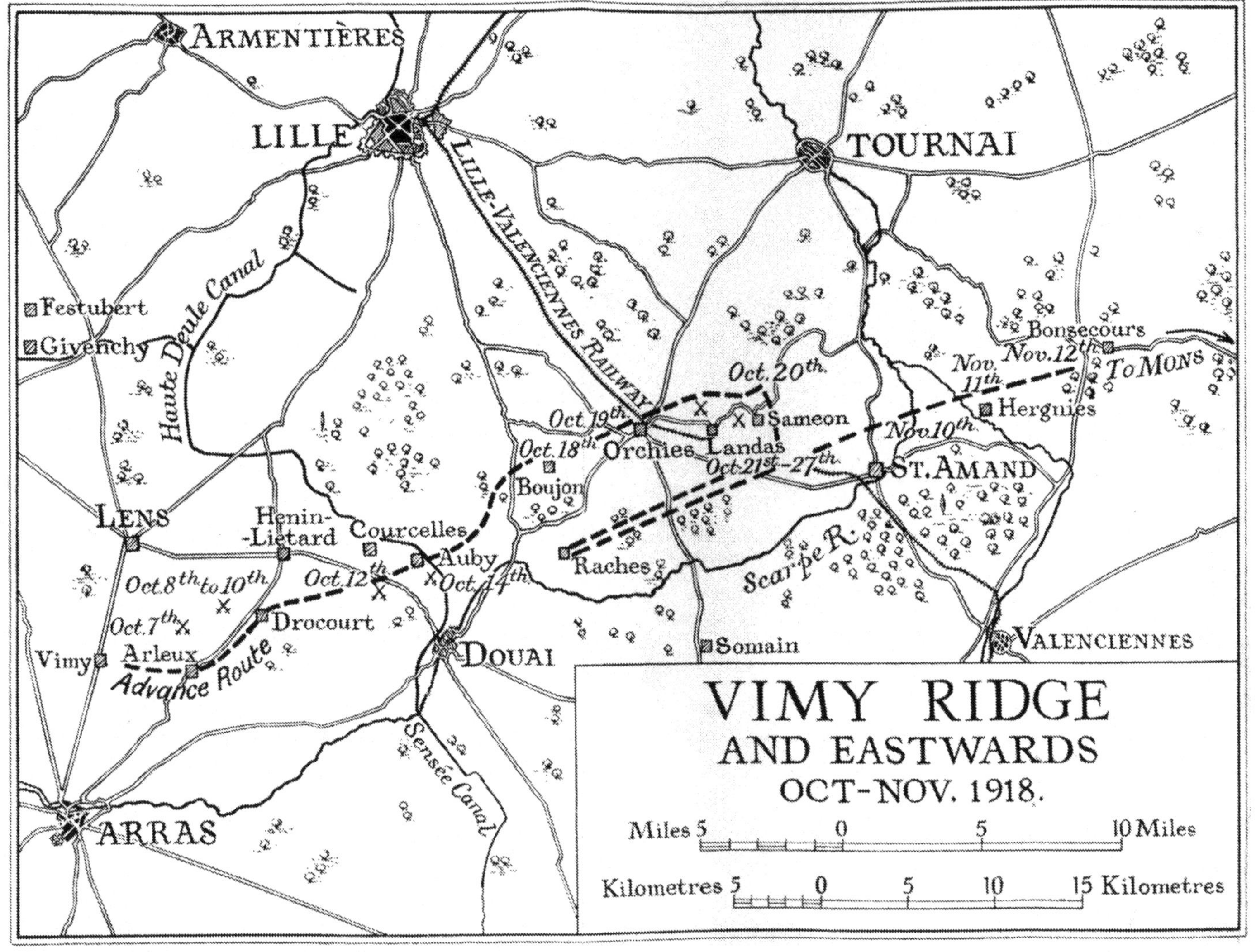

From the map prepared by Brigadier-General Riddell and Colonel Clayton to illustrate their later account of the history of the Cambridgeshires from 1914 to 1919. Sergeant Stanley indicates he was at Vimy with the Army Ordnance Corps.

others stranded just as their teams were shot down or fled from this avenging army. It is rather ironical that large quantities of Lewis Guns which the Germans captured from us in the spring have so soon been converted to use their ammunition are now being left behind and turned upon them again.

Every day now we are sending over leaflets telling the already hard-pressed German troops of their plight, and judging by events along the front they do not want much convincing. These leaflets are sent over in a steady stream when the wind is right from miniature hydrogen-filled balloons with time dropping devices. The Kaiser apparently still holds sway over his satellites for everywhere chalked in block letters one finds the words HOCK-DER-KAISER but where our Infantry have been before one finds by a slight alteration of the first two letters a popular but most uncomplimentary phrase.

November 1918

In a dugout on Vimy Ridge, watching for bombs.

It is November now and if the advance continues we shall be in Mons in a few more days but under different conditions this time to our magnificent Army of 1914. The weather is holding things up a bit now but making it just as difficult for the enemy who appears to be confining his rearguard action to machine gunners who lurk in concealed spots and fight until their ammunition is exhausted or the teams are killed - a desperate expedient but inflicting heavy casualties on our troops. On the 10th day the well-worn rumour of an armistice travels around like wildfire and it is to happen on the 11th. It looks like it, fresh troops are being rushed up, more guns are getting into position, motor machine gunners are in readiness, it looks like one of two things - either a fresh push forward or an expected counter attack by the enemy, but an armistice, rubbish. We used to talk about these things years ago. No we are sceptics all and cannot believe in peace again and sure enough on the morning of the 11th the guns open up louder than ever, the rifles and machine guns rattle and splutter and the slaughter continues with renewed energy.

At eleven o'clock a hush falls over the land, an eerie ghostly quietness, a peculiar feeling prevails as though the clock has stopped. Not even the tramp of feet, or the rattle of transport and all the familiar sounds that had filled our brain cells for so long. We are even lost for words among ourselves. What does it mean? Are we going to let the enemy fool us after all? But he has already departed and now for the victorious march to Berlin, but alas our rulers decree otherwise and we must not hurt our enemy's feelings.

In the workshop, probably after the Armistice.

Postscript following the end of the War

The War is over and Peace returns, the peace of our beloved England, the home of our forefathers, the great and only England which means so much to us patriots.

I am fortunate and obtain employment as an artisan on this land which we have been promised will be fit for heroes to live in. I certainly am allowed to live, but not happily, for all around I see cruel suffering of the men with whom I fought side by side, men who have no jobs and so are not allowed to live, so these promises are mere idle rhetoric. The women still cling to their jobs and while the men have been fighting the youth and womanhood have ousted them in their absence. There is unrest throughout the land where the cost of living is high and there is a conspiracy to force down the reward for honest labour to a point where free men become serfs.

From the few pounds that I hardly gain a tax is levied to pay for the war. We are told that industry cannot afford to pay more. The fraudulent money bags who deal in what is called finance and talk about patriotism and the Empire, who wag the flag the most and decry the fall of the national spirit, who hoard up money at the expense of flesh and blood, but they exclaim in horror we have lost sons in the war, maybe but it has not taught them any lesson and apart from a momentary moral pang they still trade their nefarious schemes. Profits earned by the workers who deserve a share, filched and faked from revenue and used to amass capital which changes hands with colossal gain, our capitalisation whereby ridiculous profits have to earned and the poor deluded workers are told that no profit is being made, that they are slacking and must have less wages, and when they ask for fair play from these so-called Britishers who shout the most about our greatness, they squeal and threaten to remove their wealth from this country.

What has happened to this phantom army who but a year ago fought fearlessly that England might live, have they lost their dauntless courage for surely these things should not be. Why do they not rise and bury these harping hypocrites with their own filthy lucre and so once again raise the fair name of England from such mediocrity.

Here is P-K who has built up his wealth from cheap, female labour who invites the public to inspect his goods and sacks the poor assistant who lets them escape without an order, his porter a worker who has helped to amass his wealth lies dying. A few pounds would ease his exit but no, he is sacked. He is a great patriot, also a great saint with a front seat in Church. He goes round with the bag for the collection to avoid putting in a coin himself. When he does he will probably bequeath a fine window to the Church and painted upon it should be the dying porter on a cross with a crown of thorns.

A-B dies and leaves half a million pounds, he leaves fifty pounds to his good and faithful Butler as a reward for life's service. He regrets the smallness of his bequests but he lost a lot of money during the war. Poor soul. A pity he had to go and leave it all.

Another dear old soul leaves a princely fortune with a request that it shall not leave the family. What a pity if some of it got into the hands of these poor ex-soldiers but for whom she might have been penniless and every day the newspapers advertise the fact to these workless men that all these poor hard-hit poverty stricken people die and leave these enormous fortunes[7].

On the anniversary of Armistice Day there is a solemn ritual in remembrance of our dead when for two silent minutes we think of those that we loved, where parents and relatives gather together in the fullness of their sorrow. Boxes are thrust under their noses and there is a rattle of money and a request to buy tokens for a fund to help these warriors at once reducing this solemn occasion to the status of a country fair. In the proudness of their hearts they give often what they can ill afford or stay away. Now the greatness of our country sunk as low or the moral obligation of such little honour, or are ex-braggarts, is our greatness merely rhetoric and our code of honour to even our own countrymen false, if not why need this be.

Here are able-bodied men in good jobs who were called up as conscripts, who by every artifice avoided conflict with our enemies who by some subtle injustice draw good pensions for which we pay whilst many of our comrades who fought are workless and with no reward.

Here are well known and well fed faces with rich rewards, with honours with decorations for drawing good salaries, and never missing a good night in bed in safety, who raise the flag on high and talk of our power and our noble national traits, away with this humbug and whitewash and let justice balance the scales.

The bitterness towards our old enemies is disappearing. We sit with our womenfolk at lunch in a hostel under the walls of the Palace of Versailles and our conversation turns of the war. My neighbour is a German student who is war-scarred. He was wounded and taken prisoner by the Russians spending some of his captivity in Siberia. He swears there must be no more war. My other neighbour, a Frenchman, was gassed and taken prisoner by the Germans and still suffers from the war. He declares there must be no more war. An elderly Belgian opposite lived through the German occupation of his Country, losing all his sons. He prays that there shall be no more war. And yet are we not representative examples of the people who allowed this thing.

The Church is preaching the gospel of no more war, except amongst themselves, even the men who fought are preaching the gospel of no more war.

The schools are preaching the same gospel to potential soldiers and citizens. These

The last of Sergeant Stanleys photographs - he entitles it 'Comrades'.

children are taken to the Cinema and on the films they see depicted the misery, the suffering, the financial cost and figures and statistics are shown to prove the futility of war, but they are restless and uninterested and think it is a rotten show and thin sentries appear on the Rumanian frontier and they sit up and take notice. Shots are exchanged and they express delight. Troops are marching and martial music plays. They cheer, the guns boom, rifle and machine guns rattle. They clap and cheer the louder, a bayonet charge and the dead and dying soldiers lay on the field and they are uncontrollable. The film is stopped and a teacher explains that they are putting the wrong construction on this picture and that it is intended to stifle the desire for war. But this is the spirit of youth, indomitable, unquenchable, the love of adventure, honour and glory, rolling on like the ocean, carrying all before it, it cannot, it will not be stemmed and as through the ages so war will come again and when the drums roll and the trumpets blast the call will come again. It will have to be a very loud call but I suppose I shall answer it.

So mourn my fellow mortals mourn
But not with tears and sadness.
Think of the fragrant flowers that raise their heads
And give out all their gladness.
Thy loved ones have but returned to the elements by which we live
But their souls live on for ever.
So cast aside all morbid thoughts
And have a thought for others
For the dead do not return.

References

Macdonald, P. (ed.) 1998. The Cambridgeshire Regiment, a guide. Colourplan, Ipswich.

Riddell, E. & Clayton, M.C. 1934. The Cambridgeshires 1914 to 1919. Bowes & Bowes, Cambridge.

Appendix

Mr. Cliff Brown has very kindly supplied us with some information relevant to the diary. These are listed below.

On pp. 18-19 grandad mentions graves being dug near Dickebush and a Cambs man being hit in the stomach and dying and ending up at this cemetery. Cliff Brown thinks that this was the battalion's first casualty, Noble Dewey, who was buried in Dickebush New Military Cemetery.

On p. 22 there is mention of Johnny and Snob, two inseparables of the sanitary men. The sanitary men of B company, nominally attached to 5 platoon, were Sgt A. Ripley, Pte W.T. Jervis and Pte Lilley. Cliff Brown also thinks this was F.J. Lilley. He also thinks that Jervis was perhaps Snob and Lilley perhaps Johnny.

Cliff Brown also considers that the diary [or at least part - JB] was written up later because some of the timings are mixed up. Most of it runs to dates that can be identified quite easily. An instance is on p. 29 which reads, "They apparently have a strong sense of humour, but it is no joke and rather spoils the fun when a very large Sergeant who is recording for me suddenly lurched back against the back of the trench and throws up his hands to his to face which is covered with blood." This was Sgt H. Pull (standing next to grandad in the picture). This incident was on May 1st but he then goes back to April.

The incident near Hill 60, pp. 32-33, when they got cut up was on May 5th and involved several platoons of C company.

On p. 25 the man who was hit and believed to be dead was Pte A. Symonds. It happened on March 14th before the action at St. Eloi, which grandad goes on to describe in detail. The "dead man coming alive" story is repeated in another diary Cliff Brown has from another B Company man and also in a letter from Lt R. Tebbutt. Lt. Tebbutt was an officer in B Company and brother of the Second in Command Capt Oswald Tebbutt who was killed on March 14 at St. Eloi whilst making a reconnaisance of the village.

P. 8. The 3/1st battalion went to Windsor on 28th August 1915 as part of the East

Anglian Reserve Brigade and moved to Halton Park, Tring, on 10th October.1915.

Footnotes

1 Eastern Gas News
2 Sergeant Frederick Charles Stanley 26006 2nd/6th Battalion, North Staffordshire Regiment (formerly (891) Cambridgeshire Regiment).
3 The French word "Poilu" means man of mettle, especialy a French solder.
4 My father told me that there was an occasion when such a hospital ship spent three dreadful days in the Channel unable to get into harbour because of storms, but I think not on this occasion. HB.
5 Cambridge Gas Works.
6 We cannot read the word here in the original diary so have put "wearing" as a suitable option.
7 His dug-out received a direct hit somewhere near Arras, Spring 1918.
8 For a brief time my father became a Communist, but eventually he turned against it becoming a staunch Conservative! HB.

Index

Lightning Source UK Ltd.
Milton Keynes UK
UKOW04f0613240417
299766UK00012B/522/P

9 780946 148837